PRACTICAL INSIGHT MEDITATION

BASIC AND PROGRESSIVE STAGES

The Venerable

Mahasi Sayadaw

Translated from the Burmese
by
U Pe Thin and Myanaung U Tin

BUDDHIST PUBLICATION SOCIETY
KANDY SRI LANKA

PRACTICAL INSIGHT MEDITATION

Buddhist Publication Society
P.O. Box 61
54, Sangharaja Mawatha
Kandy, Sri Lanka

First published in 1971.
Reprinted: 1976, 1980, 1984, 1991.

ISBN 955-24-0089-9

Typest at the BPS using an Atari 1040ST
computer and Signum 2.0 software.
Text set in Garamond

Offset in Sri Lanka by
Felix Printers Ltd.
Colombo 10

Ven. Mahasi Sayadaw

CONTENTS

PREFACE

It is a truism that nobody likes suffering and everybody seeks happiness. In this world of ours, human beings make all possible efforts to prevent and alleviate suffering and to enjoy happiness. Nevertheless, their efforts are mainly directed to obtaining their physical well-being by material means. Happiness, however, is conditioned by attitudes of mind, and yet only a few persons give real thought to mental development, while fewer still practise mind-training in earnest.

To illustrate this point, attention may be drawn to the commonplace habits of cleaning and tidying up one's body, the endless pursuits of food, clothing and shelter, and the tremendous technological progress achieved to raise the material standard of living, to improve the means of transportation and communication, and to prevent and cure diseases and ailments. All these strivings are, in the main, concerned with the care and nourishment of the body, and it must be recognized that they are essential. However, these human efforts and achievements cannot possibly alleviate or eradicate the suffering associated with old age and death, domestic infelicity and economic troubles, in short, with non-satisfaction of wants and desires. Suffering of this nature cannot be overcome by material means; it can be overcome only by mind-training and mental development.

It thus becomes clear that the right way must be sought to train, stabilize, and purify the mind. This way is found in the Mahā Satipaṭṭhāna Sutta, a well-known discourse of the Buddha, delivered well over 2500 years ago. The Buddha declared thus:

> This is the sole way for the purification of beings, for the overcoming of sorrow and lamentation, for the destroying of pain and grief, for reaching the right path, for the realization of Nibbāna, namely, the four foundations of mindfulness.

The four foundations of mindfulness are: (1) the contemplation of the body; (2) the contemplation of feelings; (3) the contemplation of mind; and (4) the contemplation of mind objects.

Obviously, this way should be followed by those in search of happiness, with a view to getting rid of the impurities of mind, which are the cause of their suffering.

If a person were asked whether he wished to overcome sorrow and lamentation, he would surely say "Yes." Then he—indeed everybody—should practise the four foundations of mindfulness.

If he were asked whether he wished to destroy pain and grief, he would not hesitate to say "Yes." Then he—indeed everybody—should practise the four foundations of mindfulness.

If he were asked whether he wished to reach the right path and realize Nibbāna, absolute freedom from old age, decay and death and from all suffering, he would certainly say "Yes." Then he—indeed everybody—should practise the four foundations of mindfulness.

How should one practise the four foundations of mindfulness? In the Mahā Satipaṭṭhāna Sutta, the Buddha said: "Dwell practising body-contemplation, feeling-contemplation, mind-contemplation, and mind-objects-contemplation." Without the guidance of a well-qualified teacher, however, it will not be easy for an average person to practise these contemplations in a systematic manner in order to make progress towards development of concentration and insight.

Having myself undergone a most intensive practical course of Satipaṭṭhāna meditation under the personal guidance of the Most Venerable Mingun Jetavan Sayadaw of Thaton, I have imparted the technique of meditation ever since 1938 and gave personal instruction as well as guidance through books and lectures to several thousands of yogis. In compliance with the requests of those of the earlier batches, who had benefited by my personal instructions, I wrote a treatise on vipassanā or insight meditation, in two volumes, consisting of seven chapters, running to 858 pages. The treatise was completed in the year 1944 and has been published in seven editions. In all the chapters, except Chapter V, the dissertations and discussions are made with references to Pali Suttas, Commentaries, and Subcommentaries. In Chapter V, I chose to write in common language, for easy understanding by my pupils, to explain how they should begin insight meditation and then proceed step by step, stating fully the salient features, in line with the *Visuddhimagga* and other texts.

This present book is the English translation of Chapter V. The first 14 pages of the Burmese original were translated into English in 1954 by U Pe Thin, an old pupil of mine, for the benefit of those who came from abroad to our meditation centre. Pages 15 to 51 of the Burmese original were translated into English, in compliance with the wish of the Venerable Nyanaponika Mahāthera, by Myanaung U Tin, a disciple and dayaka of mine, Vice-President of Buddha Sasana Nuggaha Organization, which founded Thathana Yeiktha in 1947 and has ever since been responsible for its management. Incidentally, it may be mentioned that the area of our meditation centre, Thathana Yeiktha, is nearly 24 acres, with over 50 buildings to house the meditation teachers and yogis, monks as well as lay people, both men and women.

The Venerable Nyanaponika Mahāthera put this translation into final literary shape after we confirmed his valuable suggestions. U Pe Thin's translation was revised by Miss Mary McCollum, an American Buddhist lady, to improve the style. She practised Satipaṭṭhāna meditation under the guidance of Anagārika Munindra at the Burmese Vihara in Bodh Gaya, Bihar, India. Anagārika Munindra stayed with us for a considerable period. He sent her revision to us for perusal and approval. When done, it was forwarded to the Venerable Nyanaponika Mahāthera. This book is therefore the co-ordination and combined publication of the aforesaid two translations, with my Preface added.

Chapter V of my Burmese treatise, as mentioned earlier, was written in common linguistic style. I should like to say here that the doctrinal terms found in this book without Pali names are fully explained in *The Progress of Insight*, translated from my Pali treatise into English by the Venerable Nyanaponika Mahāthera. His book *The Heart of Buddhist Meditation* itself is a veritable mine of information and instruction on this subject of vital importance.

In conclusion, I would like to say that I deeply appreciate the services of those who have done the translations and revisions as well as of those who are responsible for the publication of this book. I urge the readers of this book not to be content with the theoretical knowledge contained therein but to apply that knowledge to systematic and sustained practice. I also express my earnest wish that they may gain insight soon and enjoy all the benefits vouchsafed by the Buddha in the preamble of the Mahā Satipaṭṭhāna Sutta.

October 1, 1970
'Thathana Yeiktha'
16, Hermitage Road
Rangoon, Burma

MAHASI SAYADAW
(Bhadanta Sobhana,
Agga Mahāpaṇḍita)

PART I
BASIC PRACTICE

Preparatory Stage

If you sincerely desire to develop contemplation and attain insight in your present life, you must give up worldly thoughts and actions during training. This course of action is for the purification of conduct, the essential preliminary step towards the proper development of contemplation. You must also observe the rules of discipline prescribed for laymen (or for monks, as the case may be), for they are important in gaining insight. For layfolk, these rules comprise the Eight Precepts which Buddhist devotees observe on holidays (*uposatha*) and during periods of meditation.[1] An additional rule is not to speak with contempt, in jest, or out of malice to or about any of the Noble Ones who have attained states of sanctity.[2] If you have done so, then personally apologize to him or her or make the apology through your meditation instructor. If in the past you have spoken contemptuously to a Noble One who is presently unavailable or deceased, confess this offence to your meditation instructor or introspectively to yourself.

The Old Masters of the Buddhist tradition suggest that you entrust yourself to the Enlightened One, the Buddha, during the training period, for you may be alarmed if it happens that your own state of mind produces unwholesome or frightening visions during contemplation. Also place yourself under the guidance of your meditation instructor, for then he can talk to you frankly about your work in contemplation and give you the guidance he thinks necessary. These are the advantages of placing trust in the Enlightened One, the Buddha, and practising under the guidance of your instructor. The aim of this practice and its greatest benefit is release from greed, hatred and delusion, which are the roots of all evil and suffering. This intensive course in insight training can lead you to such release. So work ardently with this end in view so that your training will be successfully completed. This kind of training in contemplation, based on the foundations of mindfulness (*satipaṭṭhāna*), has been taken by successive Buddhas and Noble Ones who attained release. You are to be congratulated on having the opportunity to take the same kind of training they had undergone.

It is also important for you to begin your training with a brief contemplation on the "Four Protections" which the Enlightened One, the Buddha, offers you for reflection. It is helpful for your psychological welfare at this stage to reflect on them. The subjects of these four protective reflections are the Buddha himself, loving-kindness, the loathsome aspects of the body, and death.

First, devote yourself to the Buddha by sincerely appreciating his nine chief qualities in this way:

> Truly, the Buddha is holy, fully enlightened, perfect in knowledge and conduct, a welfarer, world-knower, the incomparable leader of men to be tamed, teacher of gods and mankind, the Awakened and Exalted One.

Second, reflect upon all sentient beings as the receivers of your loving-kindness, be fortified by your thoughts of loving-kindness, and identify yourself with sentient beings without distinction, thus:

> May I be free from enmity, disease and grief. As I am, so also may my parents, preceptors, teachers, intimate, indifferent and inimical beings be free from enmity, disease and grief. May they be released from suffering.

Third, reflect upon the repulsive nature of the body to assist you in diminishing the unwholesome attachment that so many people have for the body. Dwell upon some of its impurities, such as stomach, intestines, phlegm, pus, blood.[3] Ponder these impurities so that the absurd fondness for the body may be eliminated.

The fourth protection for your psychological benefit is to reflect on the phenomenon of ever-approaching death. Buddhist teachings stress that life is uncertain, but death is certain, life is precarious, but death is sure. Life has death as its goal. There is birth, disease, suffering, old age, and eventual death. These are all aspects of the process of existence.

To begin training, take the sitting posture with legs crossed. You might feel more comfortable if the legs are not interlocked but evenly placed on the ground, without pressing one against the other.[4] If you find that sitting on the floor interferes with contemplation, then sit in a more comfortable way. Now proceed with each exercise in contemplation as described.

Basic Exercise I

Try to keep your mind (but not your eyes) on the abdomen. You will thereby come to know the movements of rising and falling in this region. If these movements are not clear to you in the beginning, then place both hands on the abdomen to feel these rising and falling movements. After a short time the upward movement of inhalation and the downward movement of exhalation will become clear. Then make a mental note, *rising* for the upward movement, *falling* for the downward movement. Your mental note of each movement must be made while it occurs. From this exercise you learn the actual manner of the upward and downward movements of the abdomen. You are not concerned with the form of the abdomen. What you actually perceive is the bodily sensation of pressure caused by the heaving movement of the abdomen. So do not dwell on the form of the abdomen but proceed with the exercise. For the beginner it is a very effective method of developing the faculties of attention, concentration of mind, and insight in contemplation. As practice increases, the manner of movement will be clearer.

The ability to know each successive occurrence of the mental and physical processes at each of the six sense organs is acquired only when insight contemplation is fully developed. Since you are a beginner whose attentiveness and power of concentration are still weak, you may find it difficult to keep the mind on each successive rising movement and falling movement as it occurs. In view of this difficulty, you may be inclined to think: "I just don't know how to keep my mind on each of these movements." Then simply remember that this is a learning process. The rising and falling movements of the abdomen are always present, and therefore there is no need to look for them.

Actually it is easy for a beginner to keep his or her mind on these two simple movements. Continue with this exercise in full awareness of the abdomen's rising and falling movements. Never verbally repeat the words *rising, falling,* and do not think of *rising* and *falling* as words. *Be aware only of the actual process of the rising and falling movement of the abdomen.* Avoid deep or rapid breathing for the purpose of making the abdominal movements more distinct, because this procedure causes fatigue that interferes with the practice. Just be totally aware of the movements of rising and falling as they occur in the course of normal breathing.

Basic Exercise II

While you are occupied with the exercise of observing each of the abdominal movements, other mental activities may occur between the noting of each rising and falling. Thoughts or other mental functions, such as intentions, ideas, imaginings, etc., are likely to occur between each mental note of rising and falling. They cannot be disregarded. A mental note must be made of each as it occurs.

If you imagine something, you must know that you have done so and make a mental note *imagining*. If you simply think of something, mentally note *thinking*. If you reflect, *eflecting*. If you intend to do something, *intending*. When the mind wanders from the object of meditation which is the rising and falling of the abdomen, mentally note *wandering*. Should you imagine you are going to a certain place, mentally note *going*. When you arrive, *arriving*. When, in your thoughts, you meet a person, note *meeting*. Should you speak to him or her, *speaking*. If you imaginatively argue with that person, *arguing*. If you envision and imagine a light or colour, be sure to note *seeing*. A mental vision must be noted on each occurrence of its appearance until it passes away. After its disappearance, continue with the Basic Exercise I by knowing, by being fully aware of each movement of the rising and falling abdomen.

Proceed carefully, without slackening. If you intend to swallow saliva while thus engaged, make a mental note *intending*. While in the act of swallowing, *swallowing*. If you intend to spit, *spitting*. Then return to the exercise of rising and falling. Suppose you intend to bend the neck, *intending*. In the act of bending, *bending*. When you intend to straighten the neck, *intending*. In the act of straightening the neck, *straightening*. The neck movements of bending and straightening must be done slowly. After mentally making a note of each of these actions, proceed in full awareness with noticing the movements of the rising and falling abdomen.

Basic Exercise III

Since you must continue contemplating for a long time while in one position, that of sitting or lying down, you are likely to experience an intense feeling of fatigue, stiffness in the body or in the arms and legs. Should this happen, simply keep the knowing mind on that part of the body where such feeling occurs and carry on the contemplation, noting *tired* or *stiff*. Do this naturally, that is, neither too fast nor too slow. These feelings gradually become fainter and finally cease altogether. Should one of these feelings become more intense until the bodily fatigue or stiffness of joints is unbearable, then change your position. However, do not forget to make a mental note of *intending*, before you proceed to change position. Each detailed movement must be contemplated in its respective order.

If you intend to lift the hand or leg, make a mental note, *intending*. In the act of lifting the hand or leg, *lifting*. Stretching either the hand or leg, *stretching*. When you bend, *bending*. When putting down, *putting*. Should either the hand or leg touch, *touching*. Perform all these actions in a slow deliberate manner. As soon as you are settled in the new position, continue with the contemplation of the abdominal movements. If you become uncomfortably warm in the new position, resume contemplation in another position keeping to the procedure as described in this paragraph.

Should an itching sensation be felt in any part of the body, keep the mind on that part and make a mental note, *itching*. Do this in a regulated manner, neither too fast nor too slow. When the itching sensation disappears in the course of full awareness, continue with the exercise of noticing the rising and falling of the abdomen. Should the itching continue and become too strong and you intend to rub the itching part, be sure to make a mental note, *intending*. Slowly lift the hand, simultaneously noting the action of *lifting* and *touching* when the hand touches the part that itches. Rub slowly in complete awareness of *rubbing*. When the itching sensation has disappeared and you intend to discontinue the rubbing, be mindful by making the usual mental note of *intending*. Slowly withdraw the hand, concurrently making a mental note of the action, *withdrawing*. When the hand rests in its usual place touching the leg, *touching*. Then again devote your time to observing the abdominal movements.

If there is pain or discomfort, keep the knowing mind on that part of the body where the sensation arises. Make a mental note of the specific sensation as it occurs, such as *painful, aching, pressing, piercing, tired, giddy*. It must be stressed that the mental note must not be forced nor delayed but made in a calm and natural manner. The pain may eventually cease or increase. Do not be alarmed if it increases. Firmly continue the contemplation. If you do so, you will find that the pain will almost always cease. But if after a time, the pain has increased and becomes almost unbearable, you must ignore the pain and continue with the contemplation of rising and falling.

As you progress in mindfulness you may experience sensations of intense pain, stifling or choking sensations, pain such as from the slash of a knife, the thrust of a sharp-pointed instrument, unpleasant sensations of being pricked by sharp needles, or of small insects crawling over the body. You might experience sensations of itching, biting, intense cold. As soon as you discontinue the contemplation you may also feel that these painful sensations cease. When you resume contemplation you will feel them again as soon as you gain in mindfulness. These painful sensations are not to be considered as something serious. They are not manifestations of disease but are common factors always present in the body and are usually obscured when the mind is normally occupied with more conspicuous objects. When the mental faculties become keener you are more aware of these sensations. With the continued development of contemplation the time will come when you can overcome them and they cease altogether. If you continue contemplation, firm in purpose, you will not come to any harm. Should you lose courage, become irresolute in contemplation and discontinue for a time, you may encounter these unpleasant sensations again and again as your contemplation proceeds. If you continue with determination you will most likely overcome these painful sensations and may never again experience them in the course of contemplation.

Should you intend to sway the body, then knowingly note *intending*. While in the act of swaying, *swaying*. When contemplating you may occasionally discover the body swaying back and forth. Do not be alarmed; neither be pleased nor wish to continue to sway. The swaying will cease if you keep the knowing mind on the action of swaying and continue to note *swaying* until the action ceases. If swaying increases in spite of your making a mental note of it, then lean against a wall or post or lie down for a while. Thereafter proceed with contemplation. Follow the same procedure if you find yourself shaking or trembling. When contemplation is developed you may sometimes feel a thrill or chill pass through the back or the entire body. This is a symptom of the feeling of intense interest, enthusiasm or rapture. It occurs naturally in the course of good contemplation. When your mind is fixed in contemplation you may be startled at the slightest sound. This takes place because you feel more intensely the effect of sensorial impression while in the state of good concentration.

If you are thirsty while contemplating, notice the feeling, *thirsty*. When you intend to stand, *intending*. Then make a mental note of each movement in preparation for standing. Keep the mind intently on the act of standing up, and mentally note, *standing*. When you look forward after standing up straight, note *looking, seeing*. Should you intend to walk forward, *intending*. When you begin to step forward, mentally note each step as *walking, walking* or *left, right*. It is important for you to be aware of every moment in each step from beginning to end when you walk. Adhere to the same procedure when strolling or when taking a walking exercise. Try to make a mental note of each step in two sections as follows: *lifting, putting; lifting, putting*. When you have obtained sufficient practice in this manner of walking, then try to make a mental note of each step in three sections: *lifting, pushing, putting;* or *up, forward, down.*

When you look at the water tap, or water pot, on arriving at the place where you are to take a drink, be sure to make a mental note *looking, seeing.*

When you stop walking, *stopping.*
When you stretch the hand, *stretching.*
When the hand touches the cup, *touching.*
When the hand takes the cup, *taking.*
When the hand dips the cup into the water, *dipping.*
When the hand brings the cup to the lips, *bringing.*
When the cup touches the lips, *touching.*
Should you feel cold at the touch, *cold.*
When you swallow, *swallowing.*
When returning the cup, *returning.*
Withdrawing the hand, *withdrawing.*
When you lower your hand, *lowering.*
When the hand touches the side of the body, *touching.*
If you intend to turn back, *intending.*
When you turn around, *turning.*
When you walk forward, *walking.*
On arriving at the place where you intend to stop, *intending.*
When you stop, *stopping.*

If you remain standing for some time, continue the contemplation of rising and falling. But if you intend to sit down, *intending.* When you go forward to sit down, *walking.* On arriving at the place where you will sit, *arriving.* When you turn to sit, *turning.* While in the act of sitting, *sitting.* Sit down slowly, and keep the mind on the downward movement of the body. You must notice every movement in bringing hands and legs into position. Then resume the prescribed exercise of contemplating the abdominal movements.

Should you intend to lie down, *intending.* Then proceed with the contemplation of every movement in the course of lying down: *lifting, stretching, leaving, touching, lying.* Then make every movement the object of contemplation in bringing hands, legs, and body into position. Perform these actions slowly. Thereafter continue with rising and falling. Should pain, fatigue, itching, or any other sensation be felt, be sure to notice each of these sensations. Notice all feelings, thoughts, ideas, considerations, reflections, all movements of hands, legs, arms, and body. If there is nothing in particular to note, put the mind on the rising and falling of the abdomen. Make a mental note of *drowsy,* when drowsy, and *sleepy,* when sleepy. After you have gained sufficient concentration in contemplating you will be able to overcome drowsiness and sleepiness and feel refreshed as a result. Take up again the usual contemplation of the basic object. Suppose you are unable to overcome a drowsy feeling, you must then continue to contemplate until you fall asleep.

The state of sleep is the continuity of subconsciousness. It is similar to the first state of rebirth consciousness and the last state of consciousness at the moment of death. This state of consciousness is feeble and therefore unable to be aware of an object. When you are awake the continuity of subconsciousness occurs regularly between moments of seeing, hearing, tasting, smelling, touching, and thinking. Because these occurrences are of brief duration they are usually not clear and therefore not noticeable. Continuity of subconsciousness remains during sleep—a fact which becomes obvious when you wake up; for it is in the state of wakefulness that thoughts and objects become distinct.

Contemplation should start at the moment you wake up. Since you are a beginner, it may not yet be possible for you to start contemplating at the very first moment of wakefulness. But you should start with it from the moment when you remember that you are to contemplate. For example, if on awakening you reflect on something, you should become aware of that fact and begin your contemplation by a mental note, *reflecting*. Then proceed with the contemplation of rising and falling. When getting up from the bed, mindfulness should be directed to every detail of the body's activity. Each movement of the hands, legs, and back must be performed in complete awareness. Are you thinking of the time of the day when awakening? If so, note *thinking*. Do you intend to get out of bed? If so, note *intending*. If you prepare to move the body into position for rising, note *preparing*. As you slowly rise, *rising*. When you are in the sitting position, *sitting*. Should you remain sitting for any length of time, revert to contemplating the abdominal movements of rising and falling.

Perform the acts of washing the face or taking a bath in due order and in complete awareness of every detailed movement; for instance, *looking, seeing, stretching, holding, touching, feeling cold, rubbing*. In the acts of dressing, making the bed, opening and closing doors and windows, handling objects, be occupied with every detail of these actions in their order.

You must attend to the contemplation of every detail in the action of eating.

When you look at the food, *looking, seeing*.
When you arrange the food, *arranging*.
When you bring the food to the mouth, *bringing*.
When you bend the neck forward, *bending*.
When the food touches the mouth, *touching*.
When placing the food in the mouth, *placing*.
When the mouth closes, *closing*.
When withdrawing the hand, *withdrawing*.
Should the hand touch the plate, *touching*.
When straightening the neck, *straightening*.
When in the act of chewing, *chewing*.
When you are aware of the taste, *knowing*.
When swallowing the food, *swallowing*.
While swallowing, should the food be felt touching the sides of the gullet, *touching*.

Perform contemplation in this manner each time you partake of a morsel of food until you finish the meal. In the beginning of the practice there will be many omissions. Never mind. Do not waver in your effort. You will make fewer omissions if you persist in your practice. When you reach an advanced stage of the practice, you will also be able to notice more details than those stated here.

Advancement in Contemplation

After having practised for a day and night you may find your contemplation considerably improved and that you are able to prolong the basic exercise of noticing the abdominal rising and falling. At this time you will notice that there is generally a break between the movements of rising and falling. If you are in the sitting posture fill in this pause with a mental note on the act of sitting, in this way: *rising, falling, sitting*. When you make a mental note of sitting, keep your mind on the erect position of the upper body. When you are lying down you should proceed with full awareness as follows: *rising, falling, lying*. If you find this easy, continue with noticing these three sections. Should you notice that a pause occurs at the end of the rising as well as the falling movement, then continue in this manner: *rising, sitting, falling, sitting*. Or when lying down: *rising, lying, falling, lying*. Suppose you no longer find it easy to make a mental note of three or four objects in the above manner, then revert to the initial procedure of noting only the two sections, *rising* and *falling*.

While engaged in the regular practice of contemplating bodily movements you need not be concerned with objects of seeing and hearing. As long as you are able to keep your mind on the abdominal movements of rising and falling it is assumed that the purpose of noticing the acts and objects of seeing and hearing is also served. However, you may intentionally look at an object, then simultaneously make a mental note, two or three times, *seeing*. Thereafter return to the awareness of the abdominal movements. Suppose some person comes into your view, make a mental note of *seeing,* two or three times, and then resume attention to the rising and falling movements of the abdomen. Did you happen to hear the sound of a voice? Did you listen to it? If so make the mental note of *hearing, listening,* and having done so, revert to *rising* and *falling*. But suppose you heard loud sounds, such as the barking of dogs, loud talking, or singing. If so, immediately make a mental note two or three times, *hearing*. Then return to your basic exercise of attending to *rising* and *falling*.

If you fail to note and dismiss such distinctive sights and sounds as they occur, you may inadvertently fall into reflections about them instead of proceeding with intense attention to rising and falling, which may then become less distinct and clear. It is by such weakened attention that mind-defiling passions breed and multiply. If such reflections do occur, make two or three mental notes, *reflecting*, and again take up the contemplation of rising and falling. If you forget to make a mental note of body, leg, or arm movements, then mentally note *forgetting* and resume your usual contemplation of the abdominal movements.

You may feel at times that breathing is slow or that the rising and falling movements of the abdomen are not clearly perceived. When this happens, and you are in the sitting position, simply carry on the attention to *sitting, touching*; if you are lying down, *lying, touching*. While contemplating *touching*, your mind should not be kept on the same part of the body but on different parts successively. There are several places of touch and at least six or seven should be contemplated.[5]

Basic Exercise IV

Up to this point you have devoted quite some time to the training course. You might begin to feel lazy after deciding that you have made inadequate progress. By no means should you give up. Simply note the fact, *lazy*. Before you gain sufficient strength in attention, concentration, and insight, you may doubt the correctness or usefulness of this method of training. In such a case turn to contemplation of the thought, *doubtful*. Do you anticipate or wish for good results? If so, make such thoughts the subject of your contemplation, *anticipating* or *wishing*. Are you attempting to recall the manner in which this training was conducted up to this point? Yes? Then take up contemplation on *recollecting*. Are there occasions when you examine the object of contemplation to determine whether it is mind or matter? If so, then be aware of *examining*. Do you regret that there is no improvement in your contemplation? If so, then attend to that feeling of *regret*. Conversely, are you happy that your contemplation is improving? If you are, then contemplate the feeling of being *happy*.

This is the way in which you make a mental note of every item of mental behaviour as it occurs, and if there are no intervening thoughts or perceptions to note, you should revert to the contemplation of rising and falling. During a strict course of meditation, the time of practice is from the first moment you wake up until you fall asleep. To repeat, you must be constantly occupied either with the basic exercise or with mindful attention throughout the day and during those night hours when you are not asleep. There must be no relaxation. Upon reaching a certain stage of progress in contemplation you will not feel sleepy in spite of these prolonged hours of practice. On the contrary, you will be able to continue the contemplation day and night.

Summary

It has been emphasized during this brief outline of the training that you must contemplate on each mental occurrence good or bad, on each bodily movement large or small, on every sensation (bodily or mental feeling) pleasant or unpleasant, and so on. If, during the course of training, occasions arise when there is nothing special to contemplate upon, be fully occupied with attention to the rising and falling of the abdomen. When you have to attend to any kind of activity that necessitates walking, then, in complete awareness, each step should be briefly noted as *walking, walking* or *left, right*. But when you are taking a walking exercise, contemplate each step in three sections *up, forward, down*. The student who thus dedicates himself to the training day and night will be able in not too long a time to develop concentration to the initial stage of the fourth degree of insight (knowledge of arising and passing away)[6] and onward to higher stages of insight meditation (*vipassanā-bhāvanā*).

PART II
PROGRESSIVE PRACTICE

The Stages of Insight

Analytical Knowledge of Body and Mind

When, as mentioned above, by dint of diligent practice, mindfulness and concentration have improved, the meditator will notice the pairwise occurrence of an object and the knowing of it, such as the rising and awareness of it, the falling and awareness of it, sitting and awareness of it, bending and awareness of it, stretching and awareness of it, lifting and awareness of it, putting down and awareness of it. Through concentrated attention (mindfulness) he knows how to distinguish each bodily and mental process: "The rising movement is one process; the knowing of it is another; the falling is one process, the knowing of it is another." He realizes that each act of knowing has the nature of "going towards an object." Such a realization refers to the characteristic function of the mind as inclining towards an object, or cognizing an object. One should know that the more clearly a material object is noticed, the clearer becomes the mental process of knowing it. This fact is stated in the *Visuddhimagga*:

> For in proportion as materiality becomes quite definite, disentangled and quite clear to him, so the immaterial states that have that materiality as their object become plain of themselves too.
>
> *The Path of Purification,* XVIII,15

When the meditator comes to know the difference between a bodily process and a mental process, should he be a simple person, he would reflect from direct experience thus: "There is the rising and knowing it; the falling and knowing it, and so on and so forth. There is nothing else besides them. The words 'man' or 'woman' refer to the same process; there is no 'person' or 'soul.'" Should he be a well-informed person, he would reflect from direct knowledge of the difference between a material process as object and a mental process of knowing it, thus: "It is true that there are only body and mind. Besides them there are no such entities as man or woman. While contemplating one notices a material process as object and a mental process of knowing it; and it is to that pair alone that the terms of conventional usage 'being,' 'person,' or 'soul,' 'man' or 'woman,' refer. But apart from that dual process there is no separate person or being, I or another, man or woman." When such reflections occur, the meditator must note, "reflecting, reflecting" and go on observing the rising of the abdomen, its falling, etc.[7]

Knowledge by Discerning Conditionality

With further progress in meditation, the conscious state of an intention is evident before a bodily movement occurs. The meditator first notices that intention. Though also at the start of his practice he does notice "intending, intending" (for instance, to bend an arm), yet he cannot notice that state of consciousness distinctly. Now, at this more advanced stage, he clearly notices the consciousness consisting of the intention to bend. So he notices first the conscious state of an intention to make a bodily movement; then he notices the particular bodily movement.

At the beginning, because of omission to notice an intention, he thinks that bodily movement is quicker than the mind knowing it. Now, at this advanced stage, mind appears to be the forerunner. The meditator readily notices the intention of bending, stretching, sitting, standing, going, and so on. He also clearly notices the actual bending, stretching, etc. So he realizes the fact that mind knowing a bodily process is quicker than the material process. He experiences directly that a bodily process takes place after a preceding intention. Again he knows from direct experience that the intensity of heat or cold increases while he is noticing "hot, hot" or "cold, cold."

In contemplating regular and spontaneous bodily movements such as the rising and falling of the abdomen, he notices one after another continuously. He also notices the arising in his mind of mental images such as the Buddha, an Arahant, as well as any kind of sensation that arises in his body (such as itch, ache, heat), with attention directed on the particular spot where the sensation occurs. One sensation has hardly disappeared than another arises, and he notices them all accordingly. While noticing every object as it arises he is aware that a mental process of knowing depends on an object. Sometimes, the rising and falling of the abdomen is so faint that he finds nothing to notice. Then it occurs to him that there can be no knowing without an object.

When no noticing of the rising and falling is possible one should be aware of sitting and touching or lying and touching. Touching is to be noticed alternatively. For example, after noticing "sitting," notice the touch sensation at the right foot (caused by its contact with the ground or seat). Then, after noticing "sitting," notice the touch sensation at the left foot. In the same manner, notice the touch sensation at several places. Again, in noticing seeing, hearing, and so on, the meditator comes to know clearly that seeing arises from the contact of eye and visual object, hearing arises from the contact of ear and sound, and so on.

Further he reflects: "Material processes of bending, stretching, and so on, follow mental processes of intending to bend, stretch, and so forth." He goes on to reflect: "One's body becomes hot or cold because of the element of heat or cold; the body exists on food and nourishment; consciousness arises because there are objects to notice;

seeing arises through visual objects; hearing through sounds, etc., and also because there are the sense organs, eye, ear, etc., as conditioning factors. Intention and noticing result from previous experiences; feelings (sensations) of all kinds are the consequences of previous kamma in the sense that material processes and mental processes take place ever since birth because of previous kamma. There is nobody to create this body and mind, and all that happens has causal factors." Such reflections come to the meditator while he is noticing any object as it arises. He does not stop doing so to take time to reflect. While noticing objects as they arise these reflections are so quick that they appear to be automatic. The meditator, then, must note: "Reflecting, reflecting, recognizing, recognizing," and continue noticing objects as usual.

After having reflected that the material processes and mental processes being noticed are conditioned by the previous processes of the same nature, the meditator reflects further that body and mind in the former existences were conditioned by the preceding causes, that in the following existences body and mind will result from the same causes, and apart from this dual process there is no separate "being" or "person"; there are only causes and effects taking place. Such reflections must also be noticed and then contemplation should go on as usual.[8] Such reflections will be many in the case of persons with a strong intellectual bent, fewer in the case of those with no such bent. Be that as it may, energetic noticing must be made of all these reflections. Noticing them will result in their reduction to a minimum, allowing insight to progress unimpeded by an excess of such reflections. It should be taken for granted that a minimum of reflections will suffice here.

When concentration is practised in an intensive manner, the meditator may experience almost unbearable sensations, such as itching, aches, heat, dullness, and stiffness. If mindful noticing is stopped, such sensations will disappear. When noticing is resumed, they will reappear. Such sensations arise in consequence of the body's natural sensitivity and are not the symptoms of a disease. If they are noticed with energetic concentration they fade away gradually.

Again, the meditator sometimes sees images of all kinds as if seeing them with his own eyes; for example, the Buddha comes into the scene in glorious radiance; a procession of monks in the sky, pagodas (dagobas) and images of the Buddha; meeting with beloved ones; trees or woods, hills or mountains, gardens, buildings; finding oneself face to face with bloated dead bodies or skeletons; the destruction of buildings and dissolution of human bodies; swelling of one's body, covered with blood, falling into pieces and reduced to a mere skeleton; seeing in one's body the entrails and vital organs and even germs; seeing the denizens of the hells and heavens, etc. These are nothing but creatures of one's imagination sharpened by intense concentration. They are similar to what one comes across in dreams. They are not to be welcomed and enjoyed, nor need one be afraid of them. These objects seen in the course of contemplation are not real: they are mere images or imaginations, whereas the mind that sees those objects is a reality But purely mental processes, unconnected with fivefold sense impressions, cannot easily be noticed with sufficient clarity and detail. Hence principal attention should be given to sense objects which can be noticed easily, and to those mental processes which arise in connection with sense perceptions.

So whatever object appears, the meditator should notice it, saying mentally, e.g. "seeing" until it disappears. It will either move away, fade away, or break asunder. At the outset, this will take several noticings, say about five to ten. But when insight develops, the object will disappear after a couple of noticings. However, if the meditator wishes to enjoy the sight, or to look closely into the matter, or gets scared of it, then it is likely to linger on. If the object is one induced deliberately, then through delight it will last a long time. So care must be taken not to think of or incline towards extraneous matters while one's concentration is good. If such thoughts come in, they must be instantly noticed and dispelled. In the case of some persons, if, while contemplating as usual, they experience no extraordinary objects or feelings, they become lazy. They must notice this laziness thus: "lazy, lazy," until they overcome it.

At this stage, whether or not the meditators come across extraordinary objects or feelings, they know clearly the initial, the intermediate, and the final phases of every noticing. At the beginning of the practice, while noticing one object, they had to switch onto a different object that arose, but they did not notice clearly the disappearance of the previous object. Now, only after cognizing the disappearance of an object, do they notice the new object that arises. Thus they have a clear knowledge of the initial, the intermediate, and the final phases of the object noticed.

Knowledge of Comprehension

At this stage, when the meditator becomes more practised, he perceives in every act of noticing that an object appears suddenly and disappears instantly. His perception is so clear that he reflects thus: "All comes to an end; all disappears. Nothing is permanent; it is truly impermanent." His reflection is quite in line with what is stated in the Commentary to the Pali text: "All is impermanent, in the sense of destruction, non-existence after having been."

He reflects further: "It is through ignorance that we enjoy life. But in truth there is nothing to enjoy. There is a continuous arising and disappearance by which we are harassed over and over. This is dreadful indeed. At any moment we may die and everything is sure to come to an end. This universal impermanence is truly frightful and terrible." His reflection agrees with the commentarial statement: "What is impermanent is painful, painful in the sense of terror; painful because of oppression by rise and fall." Again, experiencing severe pain he reflects thus: "All is pain, all is bad." This reflection agrees with what the Commentary states: "He looks on pain as a barb; as a boil; as a dart."

He further reflects: "This is a mass of suffering, suffering that is unavoidable. Arising and disappearing, it is worthless. One cannot stop its process. It is beyond one's power. It takes its natural course." This reflection is quite in agreement with the Commentary: "What is painful has no self, no self in the sense of having no core, because there is no exercising of power over it." The meditator must notice all these reflections and go on contemplating as usual.

Having thus seen the three characteristics by direct experience, the meditator, by inference from the direct experience of the objects noticed, comprehends all the objects not yet noticed as being impermanent, subject to suffering, and without a self.

In respect of objects not personally experienced, he concludes: "They too are constituted in the same way: impermanent, painful, and without a self." This is an inference from his present direct experience. Such a comprehension is not clear enough in the case of one with less intellectual capacity or limited knowledge who pays no attention to a reflection but simply goes on noticing objects. But such a comprehension occurs often to one who yields to reflection, which in some cases may occur at every act of noticing. Such excessive reflecting, however, is an impediment to the progress of insight. Even if no such reflections occur at this stage, comprehension will nevertheless become increasingly clear at the higher stages. Hence, no attention should be given to reflections. While giving more attention to the bare noticing of objects, the meditator must, however, also notice these reflections if they occur, but he should not dwell on them.[9]

The Corruptions of Insight

After comprehending the three characteristics, the meditator no longer reflects, but goes on with noticing those bodily and mental objects which present themselves continuously. Then at the moment when the five mental faculties, namely, faith, energy, mindfulness, concentration, and wisdom, are properly balanced, the mental process of noticing accelerates as if it becomes uplifted, and the bodily and mental processes to be noticed also arise much quicker. In a moment of in-breathing the rising of the abdomen presents itself in quick succession, and the falling also becomes correspondingly quicker. Quick succession is also evident in the process of bending and stretching. Slight movements are felt spreading all over the body. In several cases, prickly sensations and itching appear in quick succession momentarily. By and large, these are feelings hard to bear.

The meditator cannot possibly keep pace with that quick succession of varied experiences if he attempts to notice them by name. Noticing has here to be done in a general manner, but with mindfulness. At this stage one need not try to notice details of the objects arising in quick succession, but one should notice them generally. If one wishes to name them, a collective designation will be sufficient. If one attempts to follow them in a detailed manner, one will get tired soon. The important thing is to notice clearly and to comprehend what arises. At this stage, the usual contemplation focused on a few selected objects should be set aside and mindful noticing should attend to every object that arises at the six sense doors. Only when one is not keen on this sort of noticing should one revert to the usual contemplation.

Bodily and mental processes are many times swifter than a wink of an eye or a flash of lightning. Yet if the meditator goes on simply noticing these processes he can fully comprehend them as they happen. The mindfulness becomes very strong. As a result, mindfulness seems as if plunging into any object that arises. The object too seems as if alighting on mindfulness. One comprehends each object clearly and singly. Therefore the meditator then believes: "Bodily and mental processes are very swift indeed. They are as fast as a machine or an engine. And yet they all can be noticed and comprehended. Perhaps there is nothing more to know. What is to be known has been known." He believes so because he knows by direct experience what he has not even dreamt of before.

Again, as a result of insight, a brilliant light will appear to the meditator. There arises also in him rapture, causing "goose-flesh," falling of tears, tremor in the limbs. It produces in him a subtle thrill and exhilaration. He feels as if on a swing. He even wonders whether he is just giddy. Then there arises tranquillity of mind and along with it appears mental agility, etc. When sitting, lying, walking, or standing, he feels quite at ease. Both body and mind are agile in functioning swiftly; they are pliant in being able to attend to any object desired; they are wieldy in being able to attend to an object for any length of time desired. One is free from stiffness, heat, or pain. Insight penetrates objects with ease. Mind becomes sound and straight, and one wishes to avoid all evil. Through firm faith, mind is very bright. At times, when there is no object to be noticed, the mind remains tranquil for a long time. There arise in him thoughts like these: "Verily, the Buddha is omniscient. Truly, the body-and-mind process is impermanent, painful, and without self." While noticing objects he comprehends lucidly the three characteristics. He wishes to advise others to practise meditation. Free from sloth and torpor, his energy is neither lax nor tense. There also arises in him equanimity associated with insight. His happiness exceeds his former experiences. So he wishes to communicate his feelings and experiences to others. There arises further a subtle attachment of a calm nature that enjoys the insight associated with the brilliant light, mindfulness, and rapture. He comes to believe it to be just the bliss of meditation.

The meditator should not reflect on these happenings. As each arises, he should notice it accordingly: "Brilliant light, faith, rapture, tranquillity, happiness, and so on."[10] When there is brightness, one should notice it as "bright," until it disappears. Similar acts of noticing should be made in the other cases too. When brilliant light appears, at the beginning one tends to forget noticing and enjoys seeing the light. Even if the meditator applies mindful noticing to the light, it will be mixed with feelings of rapture and happiness, and it is likely to linger on. However, one later gets used to such phenomena and one will continue to notice them clearly until they disappear. Sometimes the light is so brilliant that one finds it difficult to make it vanish by the mere act of noticing it mindfully. Then one should cease to pay attention to it and turn energetically to the noticing of any object that arises in one's body. The meditator should not ponder as to whether the light is still there. If he does so, he is likely to see it. If such a thought arises, he should disperse it by vigorously directing his attention to that very thought.

While concentration is intense, not only a brilliant light but also several other extraordinary objects arise and may continue if one inclines to one or the other of them. If such inclination happens to arise, the meditator must notice it quickly. In some cases, even if there is no such inclination towards any object in particular, faint objects appear one after the other like a train of railway carriages. The meditator should then respond to such visual images simply by "seeing, seeing," and each object will disappear. When the meditator's insight becomes weaker, the objects may become more distinct. Then each of them must be noticed until the whole train of objects finally disappears.

One must recognize the fact that cherishing an inclination towards such phenomena, like a brilliant light, etc., and being attached to them, is a wrong attitude. The correct response that is in conformity with the path of insight is to notice these objects mindfully and with detachment until they disappear.[11]

Mature Insight Knowledge

When the meditator continues to apply mindfulness to body-and-mind, his insight will grow in clarity. He will come to perceive more distinctly the arising and disappearing of the bodily and mental process. He will come to know that each object arises at one place and in that very place it disappears. He will know that the previous occurrence is one thing and the succeeding occurrence is another. So at every act of noticing, he comprehends the characteristics of impermanence, painfulness, and egolessness. After thus contemplating for a considerable time, he may come to believe: "This is surely the best that can be attained. It can't be better," and he becomes so satisfied with his progress that he is likely to pause and relax. He should, however, not relax at this stage, but go ahead with his practice of noticing the bodily and mental processes continuously for a still longer time.[12]

With the improvement of practice and when knowledge becomes more mature, the arising of the objects is no longer apparent to the meditator. He notices only their ceasing. They pass away swiftly. So also do the mental processes of noticing them. For instance, while noticing the *rising* of the abdomen, that movement vanishes in no time. And in the same manner vanishes also the mental process of *noticing* that movement. Thus it will be clearly known to the meditator that both the rising and the noticing vanish immediately one after another. The same applies in the case of the *falling* of the abdomen, of sitting, bending or stretching of an arm or leg, stiffness in the limbs, and so on. The noticing of an object and the knowledge of its ceasing occur in quick succession. Some meditators perceive distinctly three phases: noticing an object, its ceasing, and the passing away of the consciousness that cognizes that ceasing—all in quick succession. However, it is sufficient to know, in pairwise sequence, the dissolution of an object and the passing away of the consciousness of noticing that dissolution.

When a meditator can clearly notice these pairs uninterruptedly, the particular features such as body, head, hand, and leg, are no longer apparent to him, and there appears to him the idea that everything is ceasing and vanishing. At this stage he is likely to feel that his contemplation is not up to the mark. But in fact, it is not so. Mind as a rule takes delight in dwelling on the sight of particular features and forms. Because of their absence, mind is wanting in satisfaction. As a matter of fact, it is the manifestation of the progress of insight. At the beginning, it is features that are clearly noticed first, but now their ceasing is noticed first, because of the progress. Only on repeated reflection, features appear again, but if they are not noticed the fact of dissolution reappears to remain. So one comes to know by direct experience the truth of the wise saying: "When a name or designation arises, a reality lies hidden; when a reality reveals itself, a name or designation disappears."

When the meditator notices the objects clearly he thinks that his noticings are not close enough. In fact, because the insight is so swift and clear he comes to know even the momentary subconsciousness in between the processes of cognition. He intends to do something, for instance, bending or stretching an arm, and he readily notices that intention which thereby tends to fade away, with the result that he cannot bend or stretch for some time. In that event, he should switch his attention to contemplating the occurrences at one of the sense doors.

If the meditator extends his contemplation over the whole body, as usual, beginning with the noticing of the rising and the falling of the abdomen, he will soon gain momentum, and then he should continue noticing touching and knowing, or seeing and knowing, or hearing and knowing, and so on, as one or the other occurs. While so doing, if he feels that he is either restless or tired, then he should revert to noticing the rising and falling of the abdomen. After some time, when he gains momentum, he should notice any object that arises in the whole body.

When he can contemplate well in such a spread-out manner, even if he does not notice an object with vigour, he knows that what he hears fades away, what he sees dissolves in broken parts, with no continuation between them. This is seeing things as they are. Some meditators do not see clearly what is happening because the vanishing is so swift that they feel their eyesight is getting poorer or they are giddy. It is not so. They are simply lacking the power of cognition to notice what happens before and after, with the result that they do not see the features or forms. At such a time, they should relax and stop contemplating. But the bodily and mental processes continue to appear to them, and consciousness, of its own accord, continues to notice those processes. The meditator may decide to sleep, but he does not fall asleep and yet he remains fit and alert. He need not worry about the loss of sleep, because on this account he will not feel unwell or fall ill. He should go ahead with noticing energetically and he will feel that his mind is quite capable of perceiving the objects fully and clearly.

When engaged in noticing continuously both the dissolution of the objects and the act of knowing, he reflects: "Even for the wink of an eye or a flash of lightning nothing lasts. One did not realize this before. As things ceased and vanished in the past, so will they cease and vanish in the future." One must notice such a reflection.[13]

Besides, in the midst of contemplation, the meditator is likely to have an awareness of fearfulness. He reflects: "One enjoys life, not knowing the truth. Now that one knows the truth of continuous dissolution it is truly fearful. At every moment of dissolution one may die. The beginning of this life itself is fearful. So are the endless repetitions of the arisings. Fearful it is to feel that in the absence of real features and forms the arisings appear to be real. So are the efforts to arrest the changing phenomena for the sake of well-being and happiness. To be reborn is fearful in that it will be a recurrence of objects that are ceasing and vanishing always. Fearful indeed it is to be old, to die, to experience sorrow, lamentation, pain, grief and despair." Such a reflection should be noticed and then dismissed.

Then the meditator sees nothing to depend on and becomes as it were weakened in mind as well as in body. He is seized with dejection. He is no longer bright and spirited. But he should not despair. This condition of his is a sign of the progress of insight. It is nothing more than being unhappy at the awareness of fearfulness. He must notice such a reflection, and as he continues to notice objects as they arise, one after another, this unhappy feeling will disappear soon. However, if he fails to contemplate for some time, then grief will assert itself and fear will overpower him. This kind of fear is not associated with insight. Therefore care must be taken to prevent the oncoming of such undesirable fear, by energetic contemplation.[14]

Again, in the midst of noticing objects, he is likely to find faults, in this manner: "This body-and-mind process, being impermanent, is unsatisfactory. It was not a good thing to have been born. It is not good either to continue in existence. It is disappointing to see the appearance of seemingly definite features and forms of objects while in fact they are not realities. It is in vain that one makes efforts to seek well-being and happiness. Birth is not desirable. Dreadful are old age, death, lamentation, pain, grief and despair." A reflection of this nature must likewise be noticed.[15]

Then one tends to feel that body-and-mind as the

object, and the consciousness noticing it, are very crude, low, or worthless. By noticing their arising and disappearing he gets sick of them. He might see his own body decaying and decomposing. He looks upon it as being very fragile.

At this stage, while the meditator is noticing all that arises in his body-and-mind, he is getting disgusted with it. Although he cognizes clearly their dissolution by a series of good noticings he is no longer alert and bright. His contemplation is associated with disgust. So he becomes lazy to contemplate. But nevertheless he cannot refrain from contemplating. For example, it is like one who feels disgusted at every step when he has to walk on a muddy and dirty path and yet he cannot stop going. He cannot help but go on. At this time, he sees the human abode as being subject to the process of dissolution, and he does not relish the prospect of being reborn as a human being, man or woman, king or multi-millionaire. He has the same feelings towards the celestial abodes.[16]

When through this knowledge he feels disgusted with regard to every formation noticed, there will arise in him a desire to forsake these formations or be delivered from them.[17] Seeing, hearing, touching, reflecting, standing, sitting, bending, stretching, noticing—he wishes to get rid of them all. He should notice this wishing. He now longs for the liberation from bodily and mental processes. He reflects: "Every time I notice them, I am meeting with repetitions, which are all bad. I had better stop noticing them." He should take notice of such a reflection.

Some meditators, when so reflecting, actually stop noticing the formations. Although they do so, the formations do not stop taking place, namely: rising, falling, bending, stretching, intending, and so on. They go on as ever. Noticing of the distinct formations also continues. So, reflecting thus, he feels pleased: "Although I stop noticing the body-and-mind, formations are taking place all the same. They are arising, and consciousness of them is there, by itself. So liberation from them cannot be achieved by merely stopping to notice them. They cannot be forsaken in this way. By noticing them as usual, the three characteristics of life will be fully comprehended and then, no heed being given to them, equanimity will be gained. The end of these formations, Nibbāna, will be realized. Peace and bliss will come." So reflecting with delight, he continues to notice the formations. In the case of those meditators who are not capable of reflecting in this way, they continue their meditation once they become satisfied with the explanation of their teachers.

Soon after continuing meditation they gain momentum, and at that time usually various painful feelings arise in some cases. This need not cause despair. It is only the manifestation of the characteristic inherent in this mass of suffering, as stated in the Commentary thus: "Seeing the five aggregates as painful, as a disease, as a boil, as a dart, as a calamity, as an affliction, etc." If such painful feelings are not experienced, one of the forty characteristics of impermanence, suffering or no-self will be apparent at every noticing.[18] Although the meditator is properly noticing he feels that he is not doing well. He thinks that the consciousness of noticing and the object noticed are not close enough. This is because he is too eager to comprehend fully the nature of the three characteristics.

Not satisfied with his contemplation he changes his posture often. While sitting he thinks he will do better walking. While walking he wants to resume sitting. After he has sat down he changes the position of his limbs. He wants to go to another place; he wants to lie down. Although he makes these changes he cannot remain long in one particular position. Again, he becomes restless. But he should not despair. All this happens because he has come to realize the true nature of the formations, and also because he has not yet acquired the "knowledge of equanimity about formations." He is doing well and yet he feels otherwise. He should try to adhere to one posture, and he will find that he is comfortable in that posture. Continuing to notice the formations energetically, his mind will gradually become composed and bright. In the end his restless feelings will disappear totally.[19]

When the "knowledge of equanimity about formations" becomes mature, the mind will be very clear and able to notice the formations very lucidly.[20] Noticing runs smoothly as if no effort is required. Subtle formations, too, are noticed without effort. The true characteristics of impermanence, pain, and no-self are becoming evident without any reflection. Attention is directed to a particular spot at any part of the body wherever a sensation occurs, but the feeling of touch is as smooth as that of cotton wool. Sometimes the objects to be noticed in the whole body are so many that noticing has to be accelerated. Both body and mind appear to be pulling upwards. The objects being noticed become sparse and one can notice them easily and calmly. Sometimes the bodily formations disappear altogether leaving only the mental formations. Then the meditator will experience within himself a feeling of rapture as if enjoying a shower of tiny particles of water. He is also suffused with serenity. He might also see brightness like a clear sky. These marked experiences, however, do not influence him excessively. He is not overjoyed. But he still enjoys them. He must notice this enjoyment. He must also notice rapture, serenity, and bright light. If they do not vanish when being noticed, he should pay no heed to them and notice any other object that arises.

At this stage he becomes satisfied with the knowledge that there is no I, mine, he, or his, and that only formations arise; formations only are cognizing formations. He also finds delight in noticing the objects one after another. He is not tired of noticing them for a long time. He is free from painful feelings. So whatever posture he chooses he can retain it long. Either sitting or lying he can go on contemplating for two or three hours without experiencing any discomfort, spending his time tirelessly. Intending to contemplate for a while, he may go on for two or three hours. Even after that time his posture is as firm as before.

At times formations arise swiftly and he notices them well. Then he may become anxious as to what would happen to him. He should notice such an anxiety. He feels he is doing well. He should notice this feeling. He looks forward to the progress of insight. He should notice this anticipation. He should notice steadily whatever arises. He should not put forth a special effort nor relax. In some cases, because of the anxiety, joy, attachment, or anticipation, noticing becomes lax and slips back. Some who think that the goal is very near contemplate with great energy. While doing so, noticing becomes lax and they slip back. This happens because a restless mind cannot concentrate properly on formations. So when noticing is going well the meditator must go on steadily: that means he should neither relax nor put forth special effort. If he does go on steadily, he will rapidly gain insight into the end of all the formations and realize Nibbāna. In the case of some meditators, they may, at this stage, rise higher and again fall several times. They should not give way to despair but instead hold fast to determination. Heed must be paid also to noticing whatever arises at all the six sense doors. However, when noticing goes on smoothly and calmly, contemplation in such a diversified manner is not possible. So this manner of noticing should begin with gaining momentum in contemplation until it becomes smooth and calm.

If the meditator begins either with rising and falling of the abdomen, or with any other bodily or mental object, he will find that he gains momentum. And then the noticing will go on of its own accord smoothly and calmly. It will appear to him that he is watching with ease the ceasing and vanishing of the formations in a clear manner. At this point his mind is quite free from all the defilements.

However pleasant and inviting an object may be, it is no longer so to him. Again, however loathsome an object may be, it is no longer so to him. He simply sees, hears, smells, tastes, feels a touch, or cognizes. With six kinds of equanimity described in the texts he notices all the formations. He is not even aware of the length of time he is engaged in contemplation. Nor does he reflect in any manner. But if he does not develop sufficient progress of insight to gain the "knowledge of the path and its fruition" (*magga* and *phala*) within two or three hours, concentration becomes slack and reflection sets in.

On the other hand, if he is making good progress, he may anticipate further advance. He will become so delighted with the result that he will experience a "fall." Then he must dispel such an anticipation or reflection by directing bare noticing to it. A steady contemplation will achieve smooth progress again. But if sufficient strength of insight has not yet been achieved, concentration becomes slack again. In this way, some meditators progress and fall back several times. Those who are acquainted with the stages of the progress of insight by way of study (or by hearing about them) encounter such ups and downs. Hence it is not good for a pupil who meditates under the guidance of a teacher to get acquainted with these stages before meditation begins. But for the benefit of those who have to practise without the guidance of an experienced teacher, these stages have been indicated here.

In spite of such fluctuation in his progress the meditator must not allow himself to be overcome by disappointment or despair. He is now, as it were, at the threshold of the path and fruit. As soon as the five faculties (*indriya*) of faith, energy, mindfulness, concentration, and wisdom are developed in an even manner, he will soon reach the path and fruit and realize Nibbāna.[21]

How Nibbāna is Realized

Path Knowledge

The ups and downs of insight knowledge occurring in the aforesaid manner are comparable to a bird let loose from a sea-going ship. In ancient times the captain of a sea-going ship, finding it difficult to know whether the ship was approaching land, released a bird that he had taken with him. The bird flew in all four directions to look for the shore. Whenever it could not find any land, it came back to the ship. So long as insight knowledge is not mature enough to grow into path and fruition knowledge and thereby attain to the realization of Nibbāna, it becomes lax and retarded, just as the bird returns to the ship.

When the bird sees land, it flies on in that direction without returning to the ship. Similarly, when insight knowledge is mature, having become keen, strong, and lucid, it will understand one of the formations at one of the six sense doors as being impermanent or painful or without self. That act of noticing any one characteristic out of the three, which has a higher degree of lucidity and strength in its perfect understanding, becomes faster, and manifests itself three or four times in rapid succession. Immediately after the last consciousness in this series of accelerated noticing has ceased, path and fruition (*magga-phala*) arises realizing Nibbāna, the cessation of all formations.

The acts of noticing are now more lucid than the previous ones immediately before the realization. After the last act of noticing, the cessation of the formations and realization of Nibbāna become manifest. That is why those who have realized Nibbāna have said:

> The objects noticed and the consciousness noticing them cease altogether; or the objects and the acts of noticing are cut off as a creeper is cut by a knife; or the objects and the acts of noticing fall off as if one is relieved of a heavy load; or the objects and the acts of

> noticing break away as if something one is holding breaks asunder; or the objects and the acts of noticing are suddenly freed as if from a prison; or the objects and the acts of noticing are blown off as if a candle is suddenly extinguished; or they disappear as if darkness is suddenly replaced by light; or they are released as if freed from an embroilment; or they sink as if in water; or they abruptly stop as if a person running were stopped by a violent push; or they cease altogether.

The duration of realizing the cessation of formations is, however, not long. It is so short that it lasts just for an instant of noticing. Then the meditator reviews what has occurred. He knows that the cessation of the material processes noticed, and the mental processes noticing them, is the realization of path, fruit, and Nibbāna. Those who are well informed know that the cessation of the formations is Nibbāna, and the realization of cessation and bliss is the path and fruit. They would say inwardly: "I have now realized Nibbāna and have attained the path and fruit of stream-entry (*sotāpatti-magga-phala*)." Such a clear knowledge is evident to one who has studied the scriptures or heard sermons on this subject.[22]

Some meditators review defilements, i.e. those already abandoned and those remaining to be abandoned. After having reviewed in this way, they still continue the practice of noticing bodily and mental processes. While doing so, however, the bodily and mental processes appear to be coarse. Both the arising and the passing away of the processes are clearly evident to the meditator. And yet the meditator now feels as if his noticing is lax and has regressed. As a matter of fact he has come back to the knowledge of arising and passing away. It is true, his noticing has become lax and regressed. Because he has come back to this stage, he is likely to see bright lights or shapes of objects. In some cases, this reversion results in unbalanced contemplation in that the objects noticed and acts of noticing do not go together. Some meditators experience slight pain for a while. By and large, the meditators notice that their mental processes are clear and bright. At this stage, the meditator feels that his mind is absolutely free from any encumbrance; he feels happily unhindered. In such a frame of mind he cannot notice the mental process, and even if he does so, he cannot notice it distinctly. He cannot think of any other thing either. He simply feels bright and blissful.

When this feeling loses its vigour he can again notice the bodily and mental processes and know their arising and passing away clearly. After some time he reaches the stage where he can notice the formations smoothly and calmly. Then, if the insight knowledge is mature, he can again attain to the "knowledge of the cessation of the formations." If the power of concentration is keen and firm, then such knowledge can repeat itself frequently. At these times, the object of the meditators is to attain to the knowledge of the first path and fruit, and consequently they regain that knowledge repeatedly.

Thus far I have described the method of meditation, the progressive stages of insight knowledge, and the realization of the path and fruition of stream-entry.

One who has attained the knowledge of path and fruition is aware of the distinct change of his temperament and mental attitude and feels that his life has changed. His faith or trustful confidence in the Three Sacred Gems becomes very strong and firm. Due to this strengthened faith he also gains in rapture and serenity. There arises in him a spontaneous upsurge of happiness. Because of these ecstatic experiences he cannot notice the objects in a distinct manner even though he endeavours to do so right after the attainment of the path and fruit. However, these experiences wane gradually after some hours or days, and he will then be able again to notice the formations distinctly. In some cases, meditators who have attained the path and fruit feel relieved of a great burden, free and easy, and do not wish to go on contemplating. Their object, the attainment of the path and fruit, has been achieved and their hearts' contentment is understandable.

Fruition Knowledge

If one who has attained the path and fruit wishes to attain the knowledge of fruition (*phala-ñāṇa*) and to realize Nibbāna once again, he must direct his mind towards that goal and again attend to noticing mindfully the bodily and mental processes. In the course of insight meditation it is only natural that analytical knowledge of body and mind appears first to a worldling (*puthujjana*) and knowledge of arising and passing away appears first to a noble person (*ariya*). Therefore a meditator at this stage, conscious of the bodily and mental processes, will immediately achieve knowledge of arising and passing away, followed soon by the other progressive stages of insight, up to knowledge of equanimity about formations. When this knowledge matures, the cessation of formations, Nibbāna, is reached with the resultant knowledge of fruition.

This knowledge lasts just a moment to one who has not previously made a resolve on its duration; but it may sometimes last a little longer. But in the case of those who had made a prior resolve on its duration, the knowledge of fruition lasts longer, say the whole day or night, or as long as the time resolved, as stated in the Commentaries. Likewise, in these days, in the case of those immersed in concentration and insight, fruition lasts an hour, two hours, three hours, and so on. Fruition knowledge comes to an end only when the meditator wishes to terminate it. Nevertheless, during a period of fruition knowledge lasting an hour or two, reflective moments sometimes arise, but they disappear after four or five noticings, and fruition knowledge recurs. In some cases, fruition knowledge lasts for several hours, without any interruption.

While fruition knowledge lasts, consciousness is absolutely set upon the cessation of formations known by the designation "Nibbāna." Nibbāna is a *dhamma* entirely liberated from the bodily and mental process and all mundane notions. Therefore, during the experiencing of fruition knowledge there arises no awareness of one's bodily and mental processes and of this world, nor of any other mundane sphere. One is absolutely free from the entire mundane sphere. One is absolutely free from all mundane knowledge and inclinations. There are around him all objects to see, hear, smell or touch, but he is not aware of them at all. His posture is firm. If the bliss of fruition knowledge comes while he is sitting, his sitting posture remains firm, as firm as before, without bending or sagging. However, when the process of fruition knowledge comes to an end there arises at once in him the awareness of thoughts relating to the cessation of the formations or the objects of sight, hearing, etc. Then the normal contemplation returns or buoyant feeling or reflection. At the beginning the formations appear to him to be coarse and his noticings are not vigorous enough. But in the case of those who are strong in insight, their contemplation runs as smoothly as ever.

A note of warning may be given here. The meditator should make a prior resolve on the speedy entrance into fruition knowledge and the duration of it. He should not turn his attention to a resolve once he has started to notice the bodily and mental processes. Before the maturity of insight is achieved, while he is doing very well in noticing the formations, he may experience "goose-flesh," yawning, trembling, and sobbing, and loose the momentum of contemplation. While the acts of noticing are gaining strength, he may look forward to the goal and thereby lose the grip on his contemplation. But he should not think of anything other than his contemplation, and if he does so unwittingly, he must notice the extraneous thought. Some attain to fruition knowledge only after several losses of the momentum in their acts of noticing. If one's concentration is weak, then the entry into fruition knowledge is slow, and when it comes it does not last long.

This is a description of the process of fruition knowledge.

Reviewing

Some meditators pass quickly through the stages of the knowledge of fearfulness, misery, disgust, and desire for deliverance, and consequently have no clear view of them. So, if one wishes to review them, one should review each of them for a fixed time. For example, for half an hour or one hour one should pay heed only to the arising and passing away of the objects, with a resolve on the knowledge of arising and passing away. During that period the knowledge of arising and passing away remains intact, and there will be no further progress of insight. However, when that time is up, knowledge of dissolution arises by itself. If it does not arise then, attention should be given to dissolution with a resolve that knowledge of dissolution should persist for a certain time. During that period what has been resolved upon will occur.

On the expiry of the time fixed, the next higher knowledge will arise by itself. If it does not, he should aspire to the knowledge of fearfulness associated with fearful objects. Then knowledge of fearfulness will come together with fearful objects. Then he should turn his attention to miserable objects and knowledge of misery will arise very soon. When the mind is directed to disgusting objects it will give rise to knowledge of disgust. Getting disgusted with every noticing, knowledge of disgust will set in. Then the next stage must be thought of, knowledge of desire for deliverance. Seized with an ardent desire to be delivered from the formations, he should aspire to the relevant knowledge, and soon that knowledge will come, after some effort.

When one inclines towards the next higher stage, one will experience pains, wish to change postures, and become disturbed by a feeling of dissatisfaction, but will gain knowledge of re-observation. Then, the meditator must turn his mind to the knowledge of equanimity. The momentum of contemplation will go on until there arises smoothly the knowledge of re-observation. In this way, one will find that during the stipulated time, while one is noticing, the particular knowledge one aspires to arises and on its expiry the next higher knowledge arises, as if it were a rise of the barometer. If a review of the above-mentioned knowledges is not yet satisfactory, it should be repeated until one is satisfied. To a very ardent meditator the progress is so very swift that he may reach the stage of knowledge of equanimity about formations in a few moments, as also the stage of fruition knowledge. One who is well matured in the practice can attain to fruition knowledge while walking or having a meal.

How to attain the Higher Paths

When the meditator gets full satisfaction from the exercises to attain speedily the fruition knowledge of the first path, as also to abide therein for a long time, he should strive to attain the higher paths. He must then make an ardent wish in this manner, having determined a definite period for striving: "During this period I do not wish to experience the fruition knowledge. May there be no recurrence of that knowledge! May I attain to the higher path, the path I have not yet attained! May I reach that goal!" With this ardent wish, he should, as usual, notice bodily and mental processes.

The advantage of the determination of a definite period is that, if he so wishes, he can easily re-attain the fruition knowledge of the path already acquired. If no such time limit is made, and one goes on striving to attain to the higher path, then it will no longer be possible for one to re-attain the fruition knowledge of the lower path. In that event, if one finds that one cannot yet attain to the higher path or go back to the fruition knowledge of the lower path, one will be disturbed by a feeling of dissatisfaction and disappointment. The advantage of abandoning the wish for re-attaining the already attained fruition knowledge is the non-attainment of that knowledge during the particular period, and if there is maturity of insight, one can attain to the higher path. If the wish is not fully abandoned, then the previous fruition knowledge may set in again. Therefore full abandonment of the wish is called for during this defined period.

When one begins the contemplation with a view to attaining the higher path, the progress of insight will begin with knowledge of arising and passing away. Then the progress of insight is not the same as one makes while striving for the recurrence of fruition knowledge, but the same as the progress one makes in practising contemplation for the lower path. Brilliant light or shapes may appear as in the case of the earlier stage of knowledge of arising and passing away. One may experience pain. The distinct arising and passing away of the bodily and mental processes occur. Although it does not take long to regain knowledge of equanimity about formations while one is contemplating for the recurrence of fruition knowledge, now if insight does not mature one will have to remain long at the stages of the lower knowledges.

However, no difficulty will confront the meditator as in the case of his contemplation for the lower path. It is possible that in a day's time he may attain to one knowledge after another up to knowledge of equanimity about formations. The mental process of knowledge is much more lucid, distinct, and broad. Much keener are his experiences of fearfulness, misery, disgust, and desire for deliverance from the ills of the mundane spheres. Formerly, although it was possible to attain fruition knowledge four or five times in an hour, now, if insight is not yet mature for the higher path, knowledge of equanimity about formations goes on. Possibly it may last from a day to months or years. On the maturity of insight, distinct noticings of the formations having appeared, the realization of the cessation of formations comes with the attainment of the higher path and fruit. Then will come to him the knowledge of reviewing. He will later return to the stage of knowledge of arising and passing away with a very clear mental process. This is the description of the progress of insight leading to the attainment of the path of the once-returner (*sakadāgāmi-magga*).

Again, if one ardently wishes to attain to the third path, the path of the non-returner (*anāgāmi-magga*), one must again decide on a definite period during which one abandons fully the desire for returning to the fruition knowledge of the previous path. Then one resolves thus: "May only the progress of insight relating to the higher path come! May I attain the higher path and fruition!" And one must begin contemplating on body and mind as usual. One begins with knowledge of arising and passing away, but soon one will attain the higher knowledges one after the other up to knowledge of equanimity about formations. If insight is not yet mature, then that knowledge will linger on. When it matures, then it will reach the cessation of formations and with it the knowledge of the third path and fruition.

This is the description of the attainment of the third path and fruition, that is, of the *anāgāmi* or non-returner.

One who aspires to the fourth and final path and fruition, that of Arahantship (*arahatta-magga-phala*), must fix a period and give up all desire to re-attain to the fruition knowledge of the third path. Then he must begin to contemplate the bodily and mental processes as usual. This is the Only Way, as stated in the Satipaṭṭhāna Sutta. Beginning with knowledge of arising and passing away, soon knowledge of equanimity about formations will be attained. If insight is not yet mature, it will be slow. When it does mature, then the meditator will attain to the cessation of formations with the realization of the path of Arahantship.

In the foregoing paragraphs, the words to the effect that the progress of insight will end on the realization of the knowledge of the paths and fruitions (*magga-phala-ñāṇa*) refer only to those who have gained maturity in the fulfilment of *pāramitas* (perfections). Those who have not yet developed *pāramitās* fully will come to a standstill at the knowledge of equanimity about formations.

An important point to be noted is that, although the person who has attained the first path is likely to attain the second path soon with comparative ease, he will find it difficult to reach the third path for a long time. The reason is that the attainers of the first path and the second path are both well practised in the observance of virtue (*sīla*), in other words, they are paragons of virtue. In the case of the attainer of the third path, he must have also fully developed concentration (*samādhi*). Therefore, he is not able to attain the third path easily since he has to strive hard to develop concentration.

Though this is so, without the utmost effort to develop one's powers one cannot possibly know whether one is able to attain this path or that. In some cases, the attainment of a path comes only after a long time, and because one has to strive that long it must not be assumed that one has not yet fully developed *pāramitās*. Again, the present effort can lead to the fulfilment of *pāramitās*, to their maturation. So one should not waste time by weighing in one's mind the matter of having *pāramitās* or not.

The meditator should bear in mind the following undeniable point and put forth utmost effort to achieve his aspiration: "Even the development of *pāramitās* is not possible without effort. Granted that one has fully developed *pāramitās*, he cannot possibly attain any path without effort. Such a person can attain a path easily and speedily if he puts forth effort. If he has developed *pāramitās* to an appreciable extent, his effort will lead to their maturity and consequently he can attain the path he aspires to. At the least, he has sown potent seeds for the harvest of a path in the next existence."

Advice

In these times when the Buddha Sāsana still exists, those who are most ardent and keen to work for their own deliverance from the ills of the world and the attainment of path, fruit, and Nibbāna, which is the highest goal of vipassanā (insight) meditation, will be well advised to practise in the above way the contemplations of body, feelings, consciousness, and mental objects, otherwise called Satipaṭṭhāna meditation. It is, indeed, necessary for them.

A Special Note

The technique of insight meditation outlined in this treatise is quite sufficient for persons of fair intelligence. Such persons, having read it, should practise these contemplations with firm, keen desire, and great diligence in a methodical manner and they can be sure of progress. It must, however, be pointed out that the details of the experiences and the progressive stages of insight gone through by meditators cannot possibly be described in full in this short treatise. There still remains much that is worthy of description. On the other hand, what has been described here is not experienced totally by every meditator. There are bound to be differences according to one's capabilities and *pāramitās*. Again, one's faith, desire, and diligence do not remain constant always. Furthermore, a meditator, having no instructor and being entirely dependent on book knowledge, will be as cautious and hesitant as a traveller who has never been on a particular journey. Therefore, it is obviously not very easy for such a person to attain the paths, fruitions, and Nibbāna if he goes on striving without a teacher to guide and encourage him.

This being so, one who is really keen to meditate until he attains his goal must find a teacher who is fully qualified by his own attainments to guide him all along the way from the lowest stage of insight to the highest knowledges of path, fruition, and reviewing. This advice is quite in accord with what is stated in the Nidānavagga, Saṁyutta Nikāya: "A teacher should be sought for knowledge about decay-and-death as it really is." Should anybody be obsessed with pride: "I am an extraordinary man. Why should I learn from anyone?" he will be well advised to do away with such pride, as Poṭṭhila Mahāthera did.

In the course of contemplation, bearing in mind the following advice of the Buddha, one should make every effort to win the goal:

> No slacker nor the man of little strength
> May win Nibbāna, freedom from all ill.
> And this young bhikkhu, yes, this peerless man
> Bears the last burden, Māra's conqueror.
>
> Nidānavagga Saṁyutta, 21:4
> (*Kindred Sayings*, II, p. 188)

NOTES

1. The Eight Uposatha Precepts are abstention from (1) killing, (2) stealing, (3) all sexual intercourse, (4) lying, (5) intoxicants, (6) partaking of solid food and certain liquids after twelve o'clock noon, (7) abstention from dance, song, music, shows (attendance and performance), from the use of perfumes, ornaments, etc., (8) and from luxurious beds.

2. There are four noble individuals (*ariya-puggalā*). They are those who have obtained the paths and fruits:

   (1) The stream-winner (*sotāpanna*) is one who has become free from the first three of the ten fetters which bind beings to the sensuous sphere, namely, personality belief, sceptical doubt, and attachment to mere rules and rituals.

   (2) The once-returner (*sakadāgāmi*) has weakened the fourth and fifth of the ten fetters, sensuous craving and ill-will.

   (3) The non-returner (*anāgāmi*) becomes fully free from the above-mentioned five lower fetters and is no longer reborn in the sensuous sphere.

   (4) Through the path of Arahant one further becomes free of the last five fetters: craving for fine-material existence (in celestial worlds), craving for immaterial (purely mental) existence, conceit, restlessness, and ignorance.

   For a full explanation see *Buddhist Dictionary* by Nyanatiloka Mahāthera, or his *Word of the Buddha*.

3. The thirty-two parts of the body, as used in body contemplation, are: head hair, body hair, nails, teeth, skin, flesh, sinews, bones, marrow, kidney, heart, liver, diaphragm, spleen, lungs, intestines, mesentery,

stomach, excrement, bile, phlegm, pus, blood, sweat, lymph, tears, serum, saliva, nasal mucus, synovial fluid, urine, brain. For details of this meditation see *The Path of Purification* (*Visuddhimagga:* abbrev. Vism.) by Acariya Buddhaghosa, tr. by Bhikkhu Ñāṇamoli, VIII, 8.

4. The meditation instructor will explain the sitting position in detail. See also *The Heart of Buddhist Meditation*, by Nyanaponika Thera (Rider & Co., London), p.89.
5. Some of these points where the touch sensation may be observed are: where thigh and knee touch, where the hands are placed together, where finger meets finger, where thumb meets thumb, where the eyelids are closed, the tongue inside the mouth, the lips touching when the mouth is closed.
6. *Taruṇa-udayabbayañāna.* On the degrees of insight knowledge, see *The Progress of Insight* by the Ven. Mahasi Sayadaw (B.P.S., Kandy).
7. The preceding section describes the "analytical knowledge of body and mind" (*nāmarūpaparicchedañāṇa*), belonging to the "purification of view." See *Progress*, p.7; Vism. XVIII.
8. The preceding section refers to knowledge by discerning conditionality (*paccayapariggahañāṇa*), belonging to the "purification by overcoming doubt." See *Progress*, p.8ff.; Vism. XIX.
9. The preceding paragraphs refer to the "knowledge of comprehension" (*sammasanañāṇa*). See *Progress*, p.10ff.; Vism. XX, 6ff.
10. These phenomena are the "ten corruptions of insight," on which, see *Progress*, p.10ff.; Vism. XX,105ff. They have the character of "corruptions" only when they cause attachment in the meditator, or lead to conceit, i.e. if, in misjudging these phenomena and overrating

his achievements, he believes he has attained to the paths of sanctity. These "corruptions" occur at the stage of "weak knowledge of rise and fall." See *Progress*, p.12ff. Vism. XX,93ff.

11. This refers to "purification by knowledge and vision of what is path and not-path." See *Progress*, p.16; Vism. XX,126ff.

12. Reference is here to the "mature knowledge of rise and fall." See *Progress*, p.16; Vism. XXI,3ff.

13. "Knowledge of dissolution." See *Progress*, p.17; Vism. XXI,10ff.

14. "Knowledge of fearfulness." See *Progress*, p.19; Vism. XXI,29ff.

15. "Knowledge of misery." See *Progress*, p.19; Vism. XXI,35ff.

16. "Knowledge of disgust." See *Progress* p.20; Vism. XXI,43-44.

17. "Knowledge of desire for deliverance." See *Progress*, p.20; Vism. XXI,45-46.

18. For these forty characteristics, see Vism. XX,18f.; Paṭisambhidāmagga, Vipassanā-Kathā. In these texts, ten characteristics of impermanence, twenty-five of suffering, and five of non-self are enumerated.

19. This refers to "knowledge of re-observation (or reflexion)." See *Progress*, p.21f.; Vism. XXI,47ff.

20. "Knowledge of equanimity about formations." See *Progress*, p.22ff.; Vism. XXI,61ff.

21. On the balance of the five faculties, see *The Way of Wisdom*, by Edward Conze (Wheel No. 65/66), p.51.

22. At the suggestion of the Venerable Author, the following two references are here quoted, in explanation of the stages in the realization of Nibbāna, on the paths of stream-entry, once-returning, etc.:

1. Vism. XXI,126–27: "'One who sees Nibbāna, which merges in the deathless (in the sense of the end) realizes it ...' (Paṭisambhidā M.,I.35). The seeing of Nibbāna at the moment of the first path is *realizing as seeing* (*dassana*). At the other path moments it is *realizing as developing* (*bhāvanā*)."
2. *Aṭṭhasālinī* (*The Expositor*), tr. by Maung Tin: "Suppose a man who can see, is travelling along a path on a cloudy night. The path is obscured by the darkness. Lightning flashes and dispels the dark. In the absence of darkness the path becomes clear. This happens on a second journey, and again on a third journey. Here, like the man who can see his setting out on the path, so is the effort of insight put forth by the Aryan disciple for the stream-winning path. Like obliteration of the way in darkness is the darkness covering the truths. Like the moment when the lightning flashes and dispels the darkness is the moment when the light of the stream-winning path arises and dispels the darkness covering the truths. Like the manifestation of the way when darkness clears is the time of the manifestations of the four truths in the stream-winning path; and what is manifest in the path is known to the person who has got it. Like the second journey is the effort of insight to get the once-returning path.... Like the third journey is the effort of insight to get the non-returning path."

APPENDIX

The passages of Pali Suttas, Commentaries and Sub-commentaries relevant to the techniques of meditation outlined in this English translation of Chapter V of the Burmese original have been cited fully in several other chapters of the latter. But as they will not be within the reach of the readers of this English translation, some of them will be given below.

Techniques of Meditation

The Mahā Satipaṭṭhāna Sutta states:

1. "And moreover, bhikkhus, a brother, when he is walking, is aware of it thus: 'I walk'; or when he is standing, or sitting, or lying down, he is aware of it." (*Dialogues of the Buddha*, II, 329, para. 3)

2. "And moreover, bhikkhus, a brother, whether he departs, or returns, whether he looks at or looks away from, whether he has drawn in or stretched out (his limbs), whether he has donned under-robe, over-robe, or bowl, whether he is eating, drinking, chewing, savouring, or whether he is obeying the calls of nature—he is aware of what he is about. In going, standing, sitting, sleeping, watching, talking, or keeping silence, he knows what he is doing." (Ibid., para. 4)

3. "And moreover, bhikkhus, a brother reflects upon this very body, however it is placed or disposed, with respect to its fundamentals (i.e. the four elements)." (Ibid., p.330, para. 6)

4. "Herein, bhikkhus, a brother when affected by a feeling of pleasure, is aware of it, reflecting: 'I feel a pleasurable feeling.' So, too, is he aware when affected by a painful feeling." (Ibid., p.333, para. 11)

5. "Herein, bhikkhus, a brother, if his thought is lustful, is aware that it is so, or if his thought is free from lust, he is aware that it is so." (Ibid., p.334, para. 12)

6. "Herein, bhikkhus, when within a brother there is sensuous desire, he is aware of it, reflecting: 'I have within me sensuous desire.' " (Ibid., p.335, para. 13)

In consonance with these teachings of the Buddha, it has been stated in colloquial language thus: "rising" while the abdomen is rising; "falling" while the abdomen is falling; "bending" while the limbs are bending; "stretching" while the limbs are stretching; "wandering" while the mind is wandering; "thinking, reflecting, or knowing" while one is so engaged; "feeling stiff, hot, or in pain" while one feels so; "walking, standing, sitting, or lying" while one is so placed, etc.

Here it should be noted that walking and so on are stated in common words instead of "being aware of the inner wind-element manifesting itself in the movement of the limbs," as is stated in the Pali texts.

Rising and Falling Movement of the Abdomen

It is quite in agreement with the Buddha's teachings to contemplate on the rising and falling movement of the abdomen. Such rising and falling is a physical process (*rūpa*) caused by the pressure of the wind-element. The wind-element is comprised in the corporeality-group of the five groups of the physical and mental phenomena of existence (*khandha*); in the tactile object of the twelve bases (*āyatana*); in the body-impression of the eighteen elements (*dhātu*); in the wind-element of the four material elements (*mahā-bhūta*); in the truth of suffering of the Four Noble Truths (*sacca*). The corporeality-group, a tactile object, a body-impression, and the truth of suffering are certainly objects for insight contemplation. Surely they are not otherwise. The rising and falling movement of the abdomen is therefore a proper object for contemplation, and while so contemplating, being aware that it is but a movement of the wind-element, subject to the laws of impermanence, suffering, and unsubstantiality, is quite in agreement with the Buddha's discourses on *khandhas, āyatanas, dhātus,* and *saccas.* Relevant Pali passages will be shown in brief.

While the abdomen is rising and falling, the pressure and movement experienced thereby is a manifestation of the wind-element which is tactile, and perceiving that rightly as such is quite in consonance with what the Buddha taught, as briefly shown below.

Khandhavagga Saṁyutta states:

7. "Do you apply your minds thoroughly, bhikkhus, to body and regard it in its true nature as impermanent." (*Kindred Sayings,* III, p.45, para. 52)

8. "Bhikkhus, when a brother sees the body which is impermanent as impermanent, this view of his is right view." (Ibid., p.44, para. 51)

Mahā Satipaṭṭhāna Sutta (Khandha Pabba) states:

9. "Herein, bhikkhus, a brother reflects: 'Such is material form, such is its genesis, such its passing away.' " (*Dialogues of the Buddha,* II, p.335, para. 14)

Saḷāyatanavagga Saṁyutta states:

10. "Do you apply your minds thoroughly, bhikkhus, to tactile objects and regard their true nature as impermanent." (*Kindred Sayings,* IV, p.91, para. 158)

11. "Bhikkhus, when a brother sees tactile objects which are impermanent as impermanent, this view of his is right view." (Ibid., p.91, para. 156)

12. "But by fully knowing, by comprehending, by detaching himself from, by abandoning tactile objects, one is capable of extinguishing ill." (Ibid., p.10, para. 26).

13. "In him that knows and sees tactile objects as

impermanent, ignorance vanishes and knowledge arises." (Ibid., p.15, para. 53)

Mahā Satipaṭṭhāna Sutta (Āyatana Pabba) states:

14. "Herein, O bhikkhus, a brother is aware of the organ of touch and tangibles." (*Dialogues of the Buddha*, II, p.336, para. 15)

Majjhima Nikāya states:

15. "Whatever is an internal element of motion, and whatever is an external element of motion, just these are the element of motion. By means of perfect intuitive wisdom it should be seen of this as it really is, thus: This is not mine, this I am not, this is not my self." (*Middle Length Sayings*, II, p.93; III, p.287)

Thus it will be seen that the contemplation of the rising and the falling movement of the abdomen is in accord with the above discourse and also with the Mahā Satipaṭṭhāna Sutta (Dhātumanasikāra Pabba: Attention to Elements).

Again, the wind-element that causes the movement and pressure of the abdomen, comprised in the corporeality-group, is the truth of suffering.

Saccavagga Saṁyutta states:

16. "And what, bhikkhus, is the Ariyan truth about ill? Ill, it should be said, is the fivefold factor of grasping." (*Kindred Sayings*, V, p.36)

17. "Bhikkhus, ill, as an Ariyan truth, is to be fully understood." (Ibid, p.369)

Mahā Satipaṭṭhāna Sutta (Sacca Pabba) states to the same effect (*Dialogues of the Buddha*, II, p.337).

Starting with Materiality

An insight meditator should start with materiality, which is more easily discernible than mentality.

Visuddhimagga states:

18. "But one whose vehicle is insight discerns the four elements." (Vism. XVIII,5)

19. "And as regards those phenomena that are amenable to comprehension a beginning should be made by comprehending those among them that are obvious and easily discernible by the individual (meditator)." (Vism. XX,12)

Mahā-Ṭīkā, Visuddhimagga Commentary, states:

20. "Insight meditation begins with what is discernible. So a beginning should be made by comprehending those that are discernible. But later what is not easily discernible must somehow be made discernible and comprehended."

Depending also on the aforesaid commentarial and sub-commentarial statements, instructions are given to the meditators to begin with the rising and falling movement of the abdomen with a view to facilitating their meditation. However, when concentration has been developed, contemplation should be made on whatever arises at all the six sense doors. Instructions to this effect are also given to the meditators. As instructed, the meditators can very well carry on with their contemplation. Therefore, no doubt should be entertained whether it will be sufficient to contemplate only on the rising and falling movement of the abdomen.

Contemplation at the Six Sense Doors

Although contemplation must be made on whatever arises at any of the sense doors, it must not be accompanied by thoughts about it. Only bare attention is to be paid to what arises at one or the other of the six sense doors.

Therefore Salāyatanavagga Saṁyutta states as follows:

21. "Not impassioned is he among forms
but having seen form mindfully,
he experiences dispassionate mind
and is not stuck with clinging.

"Not impassioned is he among sounds,
smells and tastes, tangibles, dhammas.
But having (known) them mindfully
he experiences dispassionate mind
and is not stuck with clinging."

(*Kindred Sayings*, IV, p.44)

Contemplating on the rising and falling of the abdomen, one who knows its pressure and movement is "not impassioned among forms but having seen form mindfully."

Again, Saḷāyatanavagga Saṁyutta states:

22. "Bhikkhus, the all is to be fully known. What 'all' is to be fully known? The eye is to be fully known, visual objects are to be fully known, eye-consciousness is to be fully known, eye-contact is to be fully known, that weal or woe or neutral state experienced, which arises owing to eye-contact—that also is to be fully known. The ear is to be fully known, sounds are to be fully known . . . nose . . . scent . . . tongue . . . savours . . . body is to be fully known, tangibles are to be fully known . . . mind is to be fully known, mind-states are to be fully known. . . ." (Ibid., p.14, para. 5)

In the above passage "fully known" means the awareness of the material and mental arisings at the six sense doors. The awareness of the rising and falling movement of the abdomen is comprised in "things tangible are to be fully known."

23. "Bhikkhus, the eye is to be comprehended, visual objects are to be comprehended, . . . body is to be comprehended, tangibles are to be comprehended, . . . mind is to be comprehended, mind-states are to be comprehended." (Ibid., p.14, para. 5)

Insight Meditation Without Prior Jhāna

It is possible to begin straightaway with insight (*vipassanā*) meditation without having previously developed full concentration in jhāna.

Majjhima Nikāya Commentary states:

24. "Herein, some persons contemplate on the five aggregates of clinging as impermanent and so on without having previously developed tranquillity (*samatha*, i.e. *upacāra* and *appanā samādhi*). This contemplation is insight meditation."

This commentarial statement shows that it is possible to start with insight meditation without having striven to achieve access and full concentration. It has been stated that one whose vehicle is insight discerns the four elements, which also goes to show this possibility. Besides, of the twenty-one parts of the Mahā Satipaṭṭhāna Sutta, all except those dealing with mindfulness of breathing, the reflection on the repulsiveness of the body, and the nine cemetery contemplations, show the manner of insight meditation, and so it is obvious that insight meditation is possible thereby. However, as the Commentary observes that these parts deal with access concentration contemplations, it should be understood that access concentration is developed while contemplating on the postures of the body and so on, and having overcome the five hindrances, purity of mind is attained. Therefore, of the said parts, the *Visuddhimagga* treats the reflection on the material elements concerned with insight meditation, under the heading of a meditation subject called "discerning the elements" (*dhātu-vavatthāna*), and points out that while one is contemplating the four elements, the hindrances are overcome and access concentration is attained. On the strength of this commentarial statement, it should be borne in mind with confidence and firmness that while one is contemplating on either all the four elements or on one, two or three of the four, access concentration can be developed, the hindrances overcome, and purity of mind attained. It is the personal experience of those who practise meditation ardently.

Purity of Mind by Access Concentration

Abhidhammattha Sangaha states:

25. "Purity of mind is the twofold concentration of the accessory and the ecstatic stage." (*Compendium of Philosophy,* p.212)

Visuddhimagga states:

26. "The purification of consciousness, namely, the eight attainments, together with access concentration . . . ." (Vism. XVIII,1)

Mahā-Ṭīkā, Commentary to *Visuddhimagga*, states:

27. "Access concentration being like full concentration, the base of insight meditation is as well purity of mind. That is why the Commentator (the author of *Visuddhimagga*) states 'together with access concentration.'"

It is clear from both *Visuddhimagga* and *Mahā-Ṭīkā* that access concentration too is purity of mind.

Visuddhimagga again states:

28. "When ordinary people and trainers develop it, thinking 'After emerging from one of the eight meditative attainments we shall exercise insight with concentrated consciousness,' the development of absorption concentration provides them with the benefit of insight by serving as the proximate cause of insight, and so too does access concentration as a method of arriving at wide open (conditions) in crowded (circumstances)." (Vism. XI,123)

Mahā-Ṭīkā, commenting on this, states:

29. "As a method of arriving at 'wide open' means as a method of getting an opportunity, the ninth opportunity (the lifetime of the Buddha), for the benefit (of attainment of the path, fruition, and Nibbāna). To elaborate: as it is very difficult to come across the dispensation of a Buddha, a person, terror-stricken, is so very eager to gain deliverance from saṁsāra that he,

without awaiting the attainment of full concentration, begins insight meditation, basing it only on access concentration."

These two passages show most clearly that purity of mind can be attained also by access concentration, and insight meditation is possible thereby.

Khandhavagga Saṁyutta states:

30. "The five grasping groups, friend Koṭṭhita, are the conditions which should be pondered with method by a virtuous brother, as being impermanent, suffering, sick, as an impostor, as a dart, as pain, as ill-health, as alien, as transitory, empty and soulless.

"By a brother who is a stream-winner, friend Koṭṭhita, it is the same five groups of grasping that should be so pondered.

"By one who is a once-returner, . . . so pondered.

"By one who is a non-returner, . . . so pondered.

"Indeed, friend, it is possible for a virtuous brother methodically pondering these five groups of grasping, to realize the fruits of stream-winning; for a brother who is a stream-winner . . . to realize the fruits of once-returning; for a brother who is a once-returner . . . to realize the fruits of non-returning; and for a brother who is a non-returner . . . to realize the fruits of Arahantship."

(*Kindred Sayings*, III, pp.143-44)

This Discourse on Virtue shows clearly that one who is virtuous can ponder the five grasping-groups and, by so pondering, realize by stages the fruits of stream-winning, once-returning, non-returning, and Arahantship. The rising and falling movement of the abdomen is the wind-element comprised in the corporeality group. So it should be borne in mind steadfastly that the technique of meditation based on the rising and falling movement of the abdomen and the contemplation of the five grasping-groups that arise at the six sense doors is proper and right, leading up to the realization of the fruits of Arahantship.

In conclusion, special attention may be drawn to the fact that it is quite proper to contemplate on whatever is of material nature in any part of the body and that it is equally proper to contemplate on whatever is of the wind-element in any part of the body.

Pali Texts quoted in the Appendix

Abbreviations

D	Dīgha Nikāya
M	Majjhima Nikāya
S	Saṁyutta Nikāya
MC	Majjhima Nikāya Commentary
Vism	Visuddhimagga
VismC	Visuddhimagga Commentary
AbhS	Abhidhammattha Sangaha

All citations are from the Burmese-script Sixth Sangāyana editions.

1. Puna ca paraṁ bhikkhave bhikkhu gacchanto vā "gacchāmī" ti pajānāti. Ṭhito vā "ṭhito'mhī" ti pajānāti. Nisinno vā "nisinno'mhī" ti pajānāti. Sayāno vā "sayāno' mhī" ti pajānāti. Yathā yathā vā pan'assa kāyo paṇihito hoti, tathā tathā naṁ pajānāti. (D.II,232)

2. Puna ca paraṁ bhikkhave bhikkhu abhikkante paṭikkante sampajānakārī hoti. Ālokite vilokite sampajānakārī hoti. Ālokite vilokite sampajānakārī hoti. Samiñjite pasārite sampajānakārī hoti. Saṅghāṭi-pattacīvaradhāraṇe sampajānakārī hoti. Asite pīte khāyite sāyite sampajānakārī hoti. Uccārapassāvakamme sampajānakārī hoti. Gate ṭhite nisinne sutte jāgarite bhāsite tunhībhāve sampajānakārī hoti. (D.II,233)

3. Puna ca paraṁ bhikkhave bhikkhu imam eva kāyaṁ yathāthitaṁ yathāpanihitaṁ dhātuso paccavekkhati. (D.II, 235)

4. Idha bhikkhave bhikkhu sukhaṁ vā vedanaṁ vedayamāno "Sukhaṁ vedanaṁ vedayāmī" ti pajānāti. Dukkhaṁ vā vedanaṁ vedayamāno "Dukkhaṁ vedanaṁ vedayāmī" ti pajānāti. (D.II,236)

5. Idha bhikkhave bhikkhu sarāgaṁ vā cittaṁ "Sarāgaṁ cittan" ti pajānāti. . . . (D.II,237)

6. Idha bhikkhave bhikkhu santaṁ vā ajjhattaṁ kāmacchandaṁ "Atthi me ajjhattaṁ kāmacchando" ti pajānāti. Asantaṁ vā ajjhattaṁ kāmacchandaṁ "Natthi me ajjhattaṁ kāmacchando" ti pajānāti. (D.II,238)

7. Rūpaṁ bhikkhave yoniso manasikarotha. Rupāniccatañ ca yathābhūtaṁ samanupassatha. (S.II,42)

8. Aniccaññeva bhikkhave rūpaṁ aniccan'ti passati. Sā'ssa hoti sammādiṭṭhi. (Ibid.)

9. Iti rūpaṁ, iti rūpassa samudayo, iti rūpassa atthaṅgamo. (D.II,239)

10. Phoṭṭhabbe bhikkhave yoniso manasikarotha. Phoṭṭhabbāniccatañ ca samanupassatha. (S.II,355)

11. Anicce' yeva bhikkhave bhikkhu phoṭṭhabbe aniccā'ti passati. Sā'ssa hoti sammādiṭṭhi. (Ibid.)

12. Phoṭṭhabbe abhijānaṁ parijānaṁ virājayaṁ pajahaṁ bhabbo dukkhakkhayāya. (S.II,250)

13. Phoṭṭhabbe aniccato jānato avijjā pahīyati, vijjā uppajjati. (S.II,259)

14. Idha bhikkhave bhikkhu kāyañ ca pajānāti phoṭṭhabbe ca pajānāti. . . . (D.II,239)

15. Yā c'eva kho pana ajjhattikā vāyodhātu yā ca bāhirā vāyodhātu, vāyodhātu ev'esā. Tam "n'etaṁ mama, n'eso'ham asmi, na m'eso attā" ti, evam etaṁ yathābhūtaṁ sammappaññāya daṭṭhabbaṁ (M.II,85; M.III,284-85)

16. Katamañ ca bhikkhave dukkhaṁ ariyasaccaṁ? Pañcupādānakkhandhā ti' ssa vacanīyaṁ. (S.III,373)

17. Dukkhaṁ bhikkhave ariyasaccaṁ pariññeyyaṁ. (S.III,382)

18. Suddhavipassanāyāniko pana . . . catasso dhātuyo pariggaṇhāti. (Vism. II,222)

19. Ye pi ca sammasanūpagā, tesu ye yassa pākatā honti sukhena pariggahaṁ gacchanti, tesu tena sammasanaṁ ārabhitabbaṁ. (Vism. II,244)

20. Yathāpākataṁ vipassanābhiniveso'ti katvā, pacchā pana anupaṭṭhahante pi upāyena upaṭṭhahapetvā anavasesato' va sammasitabbo. (VismC. II,391)

21. Na so rajjati rūpesu, rūpaṁ disvā paṭissato, virattacitto vedeti, tañ ca nājjhosa tiṭṭhati.
Na so rajjati saddesu, saddaṁ sutvā paṭissato . . .
Na so rajjati gandhesu, gandhaṁ ghatvā paṭissato . . .
Na so rajjati rasesu, rasaṁ bhotvā paṭissato . . .
Na so rajjati phassesu, phassaṁ phussa paṭissato . . .
Na so rajjati dhammesu, dhammaṁ ñatvā paṭissato . . .
(S.II,297-98)

22. Sabbaṁ bhikkhave abhiññeyyaṁ. Kiñca bhikkhave sabbaṁ abhiññeyyaṁ? Cakkhuṁ bhikkhave abhiññeyyaṁ. Rūpā abhiññeyyā. Cakkhuviññāṇaṁ abhiññeyyam. Cakkhusamphasso abhiññeyyo. Yamp'idaṁ cakkhusamphassapaccayā uppajjati vedayitaṁ sukhaṁ vā dukkhaṁ vā adukkhamasukhaṁ vā, tampi abhiññeyyaṁ. Sotaṁ abhiññeyyaṁ. Saddā abhiññeyyā . . . Ghānaṁ . . . Gandhā . . . Jivhā . . . Rasā . . . Kāyo . . . Phoṭṭhabbā . . . Mano abhiññeyyo. Dhammā abhiññeyyā. (S.II,258)

23. Cakkhuṁ bhikkhave pariññeyyaṁ. Rūpā pariññeyyā . . . Kāyo pariññeyyo. Phoṭṭhabbā pariññeyyā . . . Mano pariññeyyo. Dhammā pariññeyyā . . . (Ibid.)

24. Idha pan'ekacco vuttappakāraṁ samathaṁ anuppādetvā va pañcupādānakkhandhe aniccādīhi vipassati. Ayaṁ vipassanā. (MC.I,113.)

25. Upacārasamādhi appanāsamādhi c'eti duvidho'pi samādhi cittavisuddhi nāma. (AbhS.)

26. Cittavisuddhi nāma sa-upacārā aṭṭha samāpattiyo. (Vism. II,222)

27. Upacārasamādhi'pi appanāsamādhi viya vipassanāya adhiṭṭhānabhāvato cittavisuddhiy'evā'ti āha "sa-upacārā" ti. (VismC. II,350)

28. Sekkhaputhujjanānaṁ sampattito vuṭṭhāya samāhitena cittena vipassissāmā'ti bhāvayataṁ vipassanāya

padaṭṭhānattā appanāsamādhibhāvanā pi, sambādhe okāsādhigamanayena upacārasamādhibhāvanā pi vipassanānisaṁsā hoti. (Vism. I,368)

29. Okāsādhigamanayenā' ti aṭṭhapaṭilābhayoggassa navamakhaṇasankhātassa okāsassa abhigamanayena. Tassa hi dullabhatāya appanādhigamampi anāgamayamāno saṁvegabahulo puggalo upacārasamādhimhi y'eva ṭhatvā vipassanāya kammaṁ karoti "Sīghaṁ saṁsāradukkhaṁ samatikkamissāmī" ti. (VismC. I,459)

30. Sīlavatāvuso Koṭṭhita bhikkhunā pañcupādānakkhandhā aniccato dukkhato anattato yoniso manasikātabbā ... ṭhānaṁ kho pan'etaṁ āvuso vijjati yaṁ sīlavā bhikkhu ime pañcupādānakkhandhe aniccato dukkhato anattato yoniso manasikaronto sotāpattiphalaṁ sacchikareyya ... sakadāgāmiphalaṁ ... anāgāmiphalaṁ ... arahattaphalaṁ sacchikareyya. (S.II,136)

ABOUT THE AUTHOR

The Venerable Mahasi Sayadaw, U Sobhana Mahāthera, was one of the most eminent meditation masters of modern times and a leader in the contemporary resurgence of Vipassanā meditation. Born near Shwebo town in Burma in 1904, he was ordained a novice monk at the age of twelve and received full ordination as a bhikkhu at the age of twenty. He quickly distinguished himself as a scholar of the Buddhist scriptures and by his fifth year after full ordination was himself teaching the scriptures at a monastery in Moulmein.

In the eighth year after ordination he left Moulmein seeking a clear and effective method in the practice of meditation. At Thaton he met the well-known meditation instructor, the Venerable U Nārada, also known as the Mingun Jetawun Sayadaw. He then placed himself under the guidance of the Sayadaw and underwent intensive training in Vipassanā meditation.

In 1941 he returned to his native village and introduced the systematic practice of Vipassanā meditation to the area. Many people, monks as well as laymen, took up the practice and greatly benefited by his careful instructions.

In 1949 the then Prime Minister of Burma, U Nu, and Sir U Thwin, executive members of the Buddha Sasananuggaha Association, invited Ven. Mahasi Sayadaw to come to Rangoon to give training in meditation practice. He acceded to their request and took up residence at the Thathana Yeiktha Meditation Centre, where he continued to conduct intensive courses in Vipassanā meditation until his death in 1982.

Under his guidance thousands of people have been trained at his Centre and many more have benefited from his clear-cut approach to meditation practice through his writings and the teachings of his disciples. More than a hundred branch centres of the Thathana Yeiktha Centre have been established in Burma and his method has spread widely to other countries, East and West.

Ven. Mahasi Sayadaw also holds Burma's highest scholastic honour, the title of Agga Mahāpaṇḍita, awarded to him in 1952. During the Sixth Buddhist Council, held in Rangoon from 1954 to 1956, he performed the duties of Questioner (*pucchaka*), a role performed at the First Buddhist Council by the Venerable Mahākassapa. Ven. Mahasi Sayadaw was also a member of the executive committee that was responsible, as the final authority, for the codification of all the texts edited at the Council.

Ven. Mahasi Sayadaw is the author of numerous works on both meditation and the Buddhist scriptures in his native Burmese. His discourses on Buddhist suttas have been translated into English and are published by the Buddha Sasananuggaha Association (16 Hermitage Road, Kokkine, Rangoon, Burma).

For further reading

THE WAY OF MINDFULNESS

Soma Thera

A translation of the Satipaṭṭhāna Sutta, the Discourse on the Foundations of Mindfulness, together with its commentaries.

Softback 155 pages

MINDFULNESS OF BREATHING

Bhikkhu Ñāṇamoli

This book brings together the most important canonical texts on the practice of mindfulness of breathing.

Softback 125 pages

THE PROGRESS OF INSIGHT

Mahasi Sayadaw

The great Burmese meditation master charts the entire development of insight meditation up to its culmination.

Softback 70 pages

THE SEVEN STAGES OF PURIFICATION AND THE INSIGHT KNOWLEDGES

Matara Sri Ñāṇārāma Mahāthera

A guide to the progressive stages of Buddhist meditation by one of Sri Lanka's most respected meditation masters.

Softback 82 pages

LIVING BUDDHIST MASTERS

Jack Kornfield

This valuable book brings to the reader the precise instructions of twelve great meditation masters, including Mahasi Sayadaw, Achaan Chah, and U Ba Khin.

Softback (ISBN 955-24-0042-2) 320 pages

All prices as in latest BPS catalog

THE BUDDHIST PUBLICATION SOCIETY

is an approved charity dedicated to making known the Teaching of the Buddha, which has a vital message for people of all creeds. Founded in 1958, the BPS has published a wide variety of books and booklets covering a great range of topics. Its publications include accurate annotated translations of the Buddha's discourses, standard reference works, as well as original contemporary expositions of Buddhist thought and practice. These works present Buddhism as it truly is—a dynamic force which has influenced receptive minds for the past 2500 years and is still as relevant today as it was when it first arose. A full list of our publications will be sent free of charge upon request. Write to:

The Hony. Secretary
BUDDHIST PUBLICATION SOCIETY
P.O. Box 61
54, Sangharaja Mawatha
Kandy Sri Lanka